QUIET TIMES
for Those Who Need COMFORT

H. NORMAN WRIGHT

HARVEST HOUSE PUBLISHERS

EUGENE, OREGON

Unless otherwise indicated, Scripture quotations are taken from the HOLY BIBLE, NEW INTERNA-TIONAL VERSION®. NIV®. Copyright © 1973, 1978, 1984 by the International Bible Society. Used by permission of Zondervan. All rights reserved.

Verses marked NASB are taken from the New American Standard Bible®, © 1960, 1962, 1963, 1968, 1971, 1972, 1973, 1975, 1977 by The Lockman Foundation. Used by permission. (www.Lockman.org)

Verses marked AMP are taken from The Amplified Bible, Copyright © 1954, 1958, 1962, 1964, 1965, 1987 by The Lockman Foundation. All rights reserved. Used by permission. (www.Lockman.org)

Verses marked TLB are taken from *The Living Bible*, Copyright ©1971. Used by permission of Tyndale House Publishers, Inc., Wheaton, IL 60189 USA. All rights reserved.

Verses marked NCV are taken from *The Holy Bible, New Century Version*, Copyright © 1987, 1988, 1991 by Word Publishing, Nashville, TN 37214. Used by permission.

Verses marked KJV are taken from the King James Version of the Bible.

Verses marked NLT are taken from the *Holy Bible*, New Living Translation, copyright ©1996. Used by permission of Tyndale House Publishers, Inc., Wheaton, IL 60189 USA. All rights reserved.

Verses marked NKJV are taken from the New King James Version. Copyright © 1982 by Thomas Nelson, Inc. Used by permission. All rights reserved.

Verses marked MSG are taken from The Message. Copyright © by Eugene H. Peterson 1993, 1994, 1995, 1996, 2000, 2001, 2002. Used by permission of NavPress Publishing Group.

Italicized text in Scripture quotations indicates author's emphasis.

Cover by Terry Dugan Design, Minneapolis, Minnesota

Cover image © Gail Shumway/Taxi/Getty Images

QUIET TIMES FOR THOSE WHO NEED COMFORT

Copyright © 2005 by H. Norman Wright
Published by Harvest House Publishers
Eugene, Oregon 97402

Library of Congress Cataloging-in-Publication Data
Wright, H. Norman.
    Quiet times for those who need comfort / H. Norman Wright.
        p. cm.
    ISBN 13:978-0-7369-1681-3
    ISBN 10:0-7369-1681-4 (pbk.)
    1. Consolation—Prayer-books and devotions—English.   2. Grief—Prayer-books and devotions—English.   3. Bereavement—Prayer-books and devotions—English.   4. Loss (Psychology)—Prayer-books and devotions—English.   I. Title.
    BV4905.3.W735 2005
    242'.4—dc22   2005001918

All rights reserved. No part of this publication may be reproduced, stored in a retrieval system, or transmitted in any form or by any means—electronic, mechanical, digital, photocopy, recording, or any other—except for brief quotations in printed reviews, without the prior permission of the publisher.

Printed in the United States of America

05   06   07   08   09   10   11   12   / BP-MS /   10   9   8   7   6   5   4   3   2   1

$\mathcal{Q}$uietness

$\sim$

It's quiet. All you hear are the sounds of silence. At times, the quiet brings a sense of relief, even a respite from whatever has occupied your mind for the past days or even weeks. For many, quietness is a welcomed visitor. For others, it means facing the pain they so furiously try to avoid. Activity has been used as Novocain to deaden the pain that has moved in as an uninvited companion.

Quietness speaks to us in many voices. It can have the voice of blame, which questions what we either didn't or did do...and wished we hadn't. Then, we feel our spirit being battered by the accusing voices.

Quietness also has a voice that brings to mind a vivid picture of the person who is no longer a part of our life. This thought overwhelms our heart and the cascade of tears begins. Perhaps that's why many fill their days with so many activities and people—because it deadens the ache.

What do most want from times of quiet? They want to hear the voice of comfort. Anyone who is hurting, struggling with sorrow, trying to cope with the aftermath of a loss, and grieving is looking for comfort. Is this you?

Comfort—a simple seven-letter word. It's a word with numerous meanings. It can mean strengthening aid, consolation in time of trouble or worry, a feeling of relief or encouragement, or easing the grief or trouble of. Is this your situation? Is it relief that you need right now? Is there some way in which you need to be encouraged? What is the grief in your life that you would like to see lifted at this time? Right now, your desire is probably for the companionship of comfort. Perhaps you're one of those who wonders if there is any comfort to be had.

You're not alone. When the devastation of life fell on Job with the loss of his children and most of what he owned, he said, "I go about mourning without comfort." The psalmist cried out to God, "When will you comfort me?"

Comfort will come and perhaps when and where you least expect it. Hold on to this knowledge—it may take your head to convince your heart that it is so. Your grief will *not* last forever. It may seem that way, but eventually it will subside.

God's Word will be one of your sources of comfort as will a touch, a word, or a prayer from others. The psalmist said, "This is my comfort and consolation in my affliction: that Your word has revived me and given me life" (Psalm 119:50 AMP).

> He heals the brokenhearted and binds up their wounds—curing their pains and their sorrows (Psalm 147:3 AMP).

> Then maidens will dance and be glad, young men and old as well. I will turn their mourning into gladness; I will give them comfort and joy instead of sorrow (Jeremiah 31:13).

> You will grieve but your grief will turn to joy (John 16:20).

Remember these words and pray them several times today,

> God, I need, I want, and I desire your comfort. Encourage me and bring others into my life to walk alongside me to hold me up. Thank you for hearing my prayer and responding. In Jesus' name, Amen.

Who Is the Keeper of Your Life?

Comfort. Sometimes it's elusive, especially when it seems the upsets and losses won't stop. They just keep coming, and there's no time to address the latest one before a new one enters your life. "Where is the relief?" you wonder. Remember, comfort means "to be encouraged." Encouragement can come from many sources— a friend calls, a card arrives in the mail, someone gives a gentle hug. It can also come from another source—God's Word. Listen to these words and promises from Psalm 121:

> I will lift up my eyes to the hills—where does my help come from? My help comes from the LORD, the Maker of heaven and earth. He will not let your foot slip—he who watches over you will not slumber; indeed, he who watches over Israel will neither slumber nor sleep. The LORD watches over you—the LORD is your shade at your right hand; the sun will not harm you by day, nor the moon by night. The LORD will keep you from all harm—he will watch over your life; the LORD will watch over your coming and going both now and forevermore.

What did you see as you read this psalm that offers you comfort?

God watches over you constantly. He doesn't sleep. He's always there. Even if you wonder where He is now, He's watching over you. He's protecting you during the day and the night. What are your nights like at this time? For many, they're the worst. You lay down and try to sleep. The more you try, the worse it gets. And your mind goes into high gear. The more you go over your scenario, the wider awake you are. Then you look at the clock and realize an hour has passed as your mind wandered. You keep saying, "I've got to sleep," but it doesn't work. The night fears and insomnia are constant companions.

Remember God's promise! He *will* protect you by night. When you're awake, follow the advice in this verse and you could be amazed by the results: "If I'm sleepless at midnight, I spend the hours in grateful reflection" (Psalm 63:6 MSG). Verses 7 and 8 can bring you comfort for the present and the future: "Because you've always stood up for me, I'm free to run and play. I hold on to you for dear life, and you hold me steady as a post."

There are four things to remember:

1. God preserves you from evil. Remind yourself of this several times today. Even if the worst happens, you won't face it alone. Life is not out of control, even if we don't understand what's happening at the moment.

2. God preserves your life, here and forever. If we have a personal relationship with Jesus Christ, our life never ends. You have the gift of eternal life.

3. God preserves you every day, not just certain days of the week. Sometimes we wonder where he was on that particular day. Have you ever said, "God is with me today at all times and in all places?" He is not limited by time and space. He knows your thoughts, feelings, and intentions. When you walk into that store or drive that car, you're not alone. Take comfort in that fact.

4. God preserves you eternally. God cares for you constantly—not on a hit-or-miss basis. There are no pauses or breaks in his caring.

If there is one thing to remember today, it is this: God is the keeper of your life—always.[1] He's watching over you, just as Eugene Peterson describes:

> The Christian life is not a quiet escape to a garden where we can walk and talk uninterruptedly with our Lord, nor a fantasy trip to a heavenly city where we can compare blue ribbons and gold medals with others who have made it to the winners' circle....The Christian life is going to God. In going to God, Christians travel the same ground that everyone else walks on, breathe the same air, drink the same water, shop the same stores, read the same newspapers, are citizens under the same governments, pay the same prices for groceries and gasoline, fear the same dangers, are subject to the same pressures, get the same distresses, are buried in the same ground.
>
> The difference is that each step we walk, each breath we breathe, we know we are preserved by God, we know we are accompanied by God, we know we are ruled by God, and therefore, no matter what doubts we endure or what accidents we experience, the Lord will preserve us from evil, he will keep our life.[2]

3

Shock's Purpose

You're shocked. The news you received wasn't good. In fact, it's hard to believe. You may even think someone made a mistake. It isn't true! It couldn't be! It's just not registering. The author of *Grieving the Loss of Someone You Love* described it well in a chapter called "God's Anesthesia":

> When we experience a great shock, as we do when we lose someone we love, that shock alters our perceptions for a time. Colors seem drab, bird songs seem out of tune—if we hear them at all. Even our favorite foods seem tasteless. The entire world seems out of focus.
>
> Often we feel numb, and any movement is an effort. We may even forget the most common elements of our lives. We may suddenly look around us at a stop sign and realize we have no idea where we are, only to discover when we really concentrate that we are mere blocks from our home. We may stand staring at someone in utter confusion, unable to remember the telephone number we have called our own for years.
>
> Such occurrences are common among the bereaved. They can be disconcerting but, if we are careful, they are seldom dangerous. Certainly, if you find yourself terribly distracted and unable to concentrate, it would be an excellent idea to arrange for others to

drive you places until you are tracking better. You will want to ask for input from people you trust when making decisions that cannot be postponed. Otherwise, you can simply "sit tight" and wait for this particular phase of your grief to pass. Be assured, it will.

There may be a few people who will interpret your shock as indifference. You may even be confused by it yourself. One woman, Margie, had a difficult time forgiving herself for being "heartless" because the afternoon of the day her mother died she took her daughter shopping for a formal to wear to the prom. Looking back, Margie could not understand why she thought clothes shopping was such an important chore that it could not be postponed. She was ashamed of herself because she had not been consumed by sorrow immediately upon hearing the news of her mother's death.

If you've had a similar experience, there's no need to feel ashamed. The fact that you functioned so well immediately following the death of your loved one does not, in any way, indicate that you are unloving or unfeeling. It is simply a reflection of the wondrous way God has provided for us to function in times of great sorrow. It may be a short while before you feel the full impact of your loss. Be grateful for that. There will be time enough to feel your pain.

The time of shock is a good time to reaffirm your faith. There may be times in the near future when you will have occasion to doubt God and his goodness. You can blunt the force of those doubts if you use this period of shock to confirm and reestablish your faith in God and the truth of his Word. Sinking your spiritual roots into the bedrock of God's Word now will allow you to remain rooted and grounded in the midst of the storm.[1]

4

Truth to Hold Onto

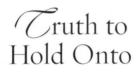

The losses that produce grief, be they the ordinary losses of life or the harsh experiences of trauma, are indeed the hardest things we will ever face. Let us remember, then, some of the truths that will help us get through the journey of grief.

Grief is a journey with a conclusion.

God has designed us with the internal ability to adjust to life's most jarring losses. That adjustment will not take place in a matter of days or even weeks if the loss was severe. Months and years are more realistic. This is not to say if a loved one dies you will not be able to cope for a very long time; rather, you will be affected and will continue to adjust your inner and outer life for a long time. We instinctively look for ways to cope from the outset, and, with God's grace, we will find ways to make it through long days and sometimes longer nights.

But with the passage of time, the journey will be completed. Sometimes we take baby steps, at other times we make longer strides. The completion of the journey does not mean that our memories are erased. Even when we approach the end of the journey, it does not mean that in future years we will not have a stab of pain when we remember the time of separation when the loss occurred. But, we will have learned how to change our lives to a new, adapted mode of living.

You don't need to go on the journey alone.

Your loss is your loss, and in that sense, you are alone. No one can truly come alongside you and say they know exactly what you are going through (although we should not be surprised when other people try to say that). However, there are people who have come through the same *kind* of thing that you have. If you lost a child, or a spouse, or a parent, or a job, or a marriage, there are others who have gone through the same journey. Most important, there are people who have made it through to the other side. Seek them out. Tell them your story. Don't expect that any one person will have all the wisdom, insight, and compassion you are craving in your loss—but do take whatever support you can from the assurances of others who have been enabled to go on with life even after being knocked to the ground.

No one can take from you the living memories, the reality of the good things you experienced with whomever you lost.

We would experience less pain if we never had anything or anyone to lose, but that would only be to our own poverty. If you are coming through the experience of grief, it is probably because there was something or someone good in your life whose absence you now are starkly aware of. That you were able to appreciate what you had is to your credit, and you carry with you into the future the same capabilities to love and to value.

If you were made a better or fuller person because of a close relationship, then you have been permanently changed for the better, and that ennobles the life of the person who is now gone.

God has offered himself to you in your grief.

God has promised that he would not leave us alone, that the lives of creatures like us who experience pain and suffering will ultimately be restored and healed if we hold onto him, and that it is possible to be reunited with those whose final destination is an eternal relationship with him. When Jesus left his disciples, he could see the pain in their eyes. He told them that they would grieve for a while, but their grief would turn to joy.

In the life of Jesus, we see God himself experiencing all of the basic kinds of loss we go through. He was betrayed by friends and rejected by those he came to help. He wept at the tomb of a friend and shook with fearful anxiety on the night before his own arrest and death. He saw people trashing their lives and making a mockery of everything that really matters to God.

But he also saw more. He saw the brilliance of the resurrection after the darkness of the tomb. He saw us, capable of standing before God clothed in righteousness. He knows us to be smoldering wicks and bent reeds. But instead of snuffing us out or breaking us, he gives us grace to go on.

When we face tragic loss, we may not feel very strong in our faith. But we must remember that faith, at its core, is the weak and troubled person throwing himself or herself on the mercy of God. And if we do so, we will find ourselves borne up.[1]

> Do you not know? Have you not heard? The LORD is the everlasting God, the Creator of the ends of the earth. He will not grow tired or weary, and his understanding no one can fathom. He gives strength to the weary and increases the power of the weak. Even youths grow tired and weary, and young men stumble and fall; but those who hope in the LORD will renew their strength. They will soar on wings like eagles; they will run and not grow weary, they will walk and not be faint (Isaiah 40:28-31).

5

ℒook Up

"Look! Look!" It's the cry of those around you who want you to see something. They don't want you to miss out. It could be a sunrise or a sunset. It could be an eagle flying high. When grief hits, most of the time we're looking down. Life goes on around us, but we don't notice very much. We soon lose our perspective. We fail to see what needs to be seen. Some say they feel "disoriented." There are many different kinds of disorientation.

For those who fly, there is an aeronautical term that is used when someone loses sight of the horizon—it's called spatial disorientation. It can be deadly. Flight-training manuals describe how this works. The eyes help determine the speed and direction of flight by comparing the position of the aircraft relative to some fixed point of reference. Eighty percent of our orientation information comes from the visual system. But sometimes disorientation occurs because of a loss of balance in the ear. And when this occurs, it's difficult for the pilot to determine if the plane is climbing, descending, or in a turn. Other factors that can lead to this disorientation are haze or a fog or a lack of a visible horizon.

Many in grief say, "It's like I'm walking around in a fog or a haze." When any loss or tragedy occurs, disorientation is likely to follow. Your senses aren't sharp. You lose your emotional balance and your sense of stability. The props are knocked out from under you. You're experiencing your own personal spatial disorientation. Up seems like down, and your life is spinning out of control. If this has been your experience, it is normal—and that's good news. The other good news is there is a way to keep from being disoriented. There is stability and balance available to you in the midst of chaos by developing a new focus.

First, practice the following:

> Do not worry about anything. But pray and ask God for everything you need, always giving thanks. And God's peace, which is so great we cannot understand it, will keep your hearts and minds in Christ Jesus. Brothers and sisters, think about the things that are good and worthy of praise. Think about the things that are true and honorable and are right and pure and beautiful and respected. Do what you learned and received from me, what I told you, and what you saw me do. And the God who gives peace will be with you (Philippians 4:6-9 NCV).

Next, "Let us fix our eyes on Jesus, the author and perfecter of our faith, who for the joy set before him endured the cross, scorning its shame, and sat down at the right hand of the throne of God" (Hebrews 12:2). The word *fix* means "to consider attentively."

In the Old Testament, the idea of fixed attention upon God and His Word meant meditation. Meditation gives a clearer focus. Hear the psalmist:

> I meditate on your precepts and consider your ways. I delight in your decrees; I will not neglect your word (Psalm 119:15-16).

> I lift up my hands to your commands, which I love, and I meditate on your decrees (Psalm 119:48).

I will meditate on all your works and consider all your mighty deeds (Psalm 77:12).

Be patient. Your disorientation will lift. You will see clearly again.[1]

6

Hold On to Hope

Everyone looks for solutions and especially quick fixes, even when it comes to the losses we experience. The questions about loss vary from "How do we get over it?" to "How do we fix it?" A better question is, "How do I live with it?" None of us have much control on when we experience loss, how often we experience it, or what our loss will be. There is one area in which we do have some control—how we respond.

Here are three suggestions that might help you:

1. Live with expectancy rather than expectations. There is a distinction between the two. Expectation tends to dictate terms to God. It insists that God do things our way and in our time frame. When we have expectations for God, we're trying to put God on our time schedule and to make changes according to what we want. But all it accomplishes is setting us up for disappointment. God doesn't operate that way because he's sovereign.

   Expectancy, however, is reasonable because it's the belief God will do something. It's being on the lookout for what he will do but with no demands. When you have an attitude of expectancy, it allows God room to do what he is going to do and when and how he will do it. As one person said, "This way we cling to the promises of God without holding Him hostage to our demands."[1]

2. Develop perspective. This comes from a number of sources and can free you up from the tunnel vision of grief. The Scriptures help us with keeping life in perspective. "Your word is a lamp to my feet and a light for my path" (Psalm 119:105). Your friends can also be a source of perspective, especially if they are good listeners and understand grief. A friend can be a sounding board and an encourager, but you need to ask for his or her help.

3. The last step is hold on to hope. When you're in grief, your focus tends to be on the past and the present. And this is understandable. It's difficult to look to the future. But hope reminds you there is a future.[2]

Hoping is desiring—you want something you don't have yet. It's also believing. You believe that what you want in the future *may* actually happen someday. But when you hope, you may also doubt because you can't be sure. There is an exception to this, however, and this can bring comfort to all of us. Lewis Smedes said, "Christian hoping is not believing in the possible, it's a confiscation about what is sure. It is a gift of certainty that what God promises he will most assuredly give. This is why Paul calls it a 'hope that never disappoints.'"[3]

The hope we have is the certainty God loves us and has provided salvation through his Son. Not only that, there is something we call "the Blessed Hope." We await and look for the Blessed Hope, even the glorious appearance of our great God and Savior Christ Jesus.

Jesus is coming again! Focusing on that will help put everything in perspective.

7

$\mathcal{V}$alleys Don't Last Forever

$\mathcal{M}$ost of us are familiar with the Twenty-third Psalm: "Even though I walk through the valley of the shadow of death, I will fear no evil for you are with me; your rod and your staff they comfort me" (Psalm 23:4). These words have become a strong source of comfort and assurance, especially when you're walking through the valley. When the psalmist wrote these words, he was thinking about those who had experienced difficult times. One version translates this, "Even if I walk through a very dark valley" (TLB).

Dark is the word many use to describe their experiences of loss. Life seems to be dark and dismal because the lights have either dimmed or gone out all together.

You didn't choose to go into that valley. I don't know anyone who would make that choice. But when you enter it, you're not entering alone even if it seems that way. "The LORD is my shepherd, I shall not be in want" (Psalm 23:1). The psalmist goes on to say:

> *He* makes me lie down in green pastures.
> *He* leads me beside quiet waters.
> *He* restores my soul.
> *He* guides me in the paths of righteousness
> (Psalm 23:2-3).

And finally he says,

> Even though I walk through the valley of the shadow of
> death, I will fear no evil, for you are with me (verse 4).

The shepherd is the one you can count on through your valley experience (and remember, it's a valley and not a box canyon. There is a way out).

One of the words that is often overlooked is in the phrase "I walk *through* the valley." Valleys don't last forever. Grief and the darkest hours don't last forever. Everyone in grief has a valley experience. It isn't permanent, although you may wonder about it. A valley is created by mountains that surround it. When you're in a valley, look up and you'll see more than the valley—that in itself should be a basis for hope.[1]

Perhaps the words of this man who lost his wife will encourage you.

> I look back now over the past several years. Sometimes I really wonder how I made it through the pain. Then I realize that I did not make it through the pain at all. God did it. "The Lord is my shepherd, I shall not want. He makes me lie down in green pastures, he leads me beside quiet water" (Psalm 23:1-2). I am back there again—in the meadows. Through Christ, I have endured the valley. That part of my life's journey is over.
>
> I may have to walk through that valley again because I have many people in my life whom I love dearly, and facing death is never easy. But God has led me through the valley once; he will do it again. I know that whether I am entering, enduring, or exiting the valley of the shadow of death, I will fear no evil. I am confident that His goodness and love will follow me all the days of my life, and I will dwell in the house of the Lord forever.[2]

8

Grief Is a New Beginning

Is grief permanent or does it have another side?" That's a question that haunts many during their grief journey. Grieving is so exhausting, tedious, unpleasant, and painful. It feels like there will never be any relief from its presence. You will get through the process and make some discoveries on the other side! You have probably heard from others by now that you need to "endure your grief." Don't endure it. Use it. Embrace it. Learn from it. Make a choice to grieve. Face it and ask, "Grief—what can I learn from you?"

What you discover may depend upon you. Some become pessimistic and sour on life. And some change their values, become more compassionate, more giving, and, in some cases, even more alive. You will be changed by your loss, but don't let it be a negative change. Hold on to the belief that grieving is an experience that can have a positive resolution. Learn from others who have experienced a positive result, and avoid those who have allowed their lives to be crippled by their grief. Grief is *not* an emotional death sentence upon your life and joy, even though there may be times when you feel that way. Throughout your life, you may revisit your grief over this loss, but it will be just a visit.

With each loss we experience, we are confronted with creating a new beginning in some way. As you read the Bible, you see new beginnings time after time. Were you aware that the grieving process is not an ending? It's a new beginning! It is an opportunity and a privilege to use it in the best way possible even though you didn't ask for it. But it is there to be used. One day you will move to the other side of grief. [1]

A friend wrote this. I pray it will give you comfort.

Mourning into Dancing

I should dance in God's presence, they say,
Though my heart is burdened with grief,
I should revel in God's mercy, they say
Though my life is shattered with pain.

A special person has died
This is the dark night of my soul.

Days and months pass on
Evenings and mornings lumber past.

My grief is great; my soul cries out,
"Why me, O God? Why me?"

"Not you my child. Not you.
Your special person has died. Not you.
I gave you life. I gave you joy.
I can give again
Sabbath.
Rest now, and begin again."

The sun burns—laughter—so slightly laughter
The pain of the grave becomes the power of grace.
Step-by-step, God works his miracle.

"You shall dance again, my child.
You shall dance again."

You, O God alone, can turn
My mourning into dancing. [2]

9

$\mathcal{D}$iscouraged?

$\sim$

Discouraged? Yes…it happens, especially when grief enters our lives. We're discouraged about our circumstances, how others respond to our progress or lack of, and the future. If I've ever heard a discouraged person, it was David from the Bible. We can identify with him. He was where many of you who are reading this book are today.

As you read this psalm, check off each phrase that describes where you are at this time in your life:

> I cry out to the LORD with my voice; with my voice to the LORD I make my supplication. I pour out my complaint before Him; I declare before Him my trouble. When my spirit was overwhelmed within me, then You knew my path. In the way in which I walk. They have secretly set a snare for me. Look on *my* right hand and see, for *there* is no one who acknowledges me; refuge has failed me; no one cares for my soul. I cried out to You, O LORD: I said, "You *are* my refuge, my portion in the land of the living, attend to my cry, for I am brought very low; deliver me from my persecutors, for they are stronger than I. Bring my soul out of prison, that I may praise Your name; the righteous shall surround me, for You shall deal bountifully with me (Psalm 142:1-7 NKJV).

Some of these descriptions are so vivid about a journey in grief. David was muffled by discouragement. Mufflers have their place. We need them on our cars to deaden the noise, and we need them around our necks to keep out the cold. But David talked about his "spirit being overwhelmed." The Hebrew words literally mean "the muffling of my spirit." When your spirit is muffled, you don't feel very alert or sharp. It's more like being disoriented. What you eat has little taste, what you do has little satisfaction...the edge of life has been taken off, and it's like walking around under a dark cloud. Daylight may be brilliant, but not for you. It wasn't for David either.

When you feel like this, you also tend to feel that no one understands or cares. This is what David is saying in verse four. People may be all around you, but you still feel alone. As you look at others laughing and carrying on in life while you're standing still, it's easy to think, "They don't have a clue. They just don't get it. They don't understand, even if they say they do. No one else can understand nor do they care."

It gets worse as we see in verse six: "I am brought very low." Desperation has hit. It's such a normal grief response. The feelings of apathy and despair will come in and out as temporary visitors. It's when they become permanent residents that trouble really begins because depression immobilizes. It will and can lift if we see it as normal and look for the reasons it is there. David stayed there a while because he began to focus on his enemies. When you're depressed, hope doesn't stay around.

But in this same psalm, David did something that was very beneficial and can help any of us. He cried out to God. He didn't mince words. He spelled it out in detail (verses 1,5,6). Do the same. You may start by saying, "God, help me!" or "God, I'm hurting!" That's a good beginning—then get specific. Express yourself aloud—write your detailed prayers to God each day for a week and read them aloud with feeling. You may be amazed at the results.

By the way, David wrote another psalm at this same time—Psalm 57. Read it and see what David found as his solution. You may be surprised.

$\mathcal{T}$he Struggle to Pray

Some days it's just difficult to pray. Neither thoughts nor words will come. And if they do, the thoughts trail off into other areas just like they do in conversations. This is what we all struggle with in the midst of our grief. When we do pray, often much of what we say centers around our loss and our grief. For years I have used the thoughts and well-crafted prayers of others to say what I am having difficulty expressing. When you are struggling, use the prayers of others to give voice to your yearning. And remember our comforter, the Holy Spirit, assists us in praying.

> Also, the Spirit helps us with our weakness. We do not know how to pray as we should. But the Spirit himself speaks to God for us, even obeys God for us with deep feelings that words cannot explain. God can see what is in people's hearts. And he knows what is in the mind of the Spirit; because the Spirit speaks to God for his people in the way God wants (Romans 8:26-27 NCV).

Read this prayer aloud today. You may want to read it several times…and perhaps you could add your own additional concerns to it as well.

O Lord God, who seest that we put not our trust in

anything that we do: Mercifully grant that by thy power
we may be defended against all adversity; through Jesus
Christ our Lord. Amen.

O God, our Father, we know that by ourselves we can
do nothing.
    If we try to face our work by ourselves,
    we collapse beneath our burdens and our responsi-
    bilities. Our bodies become exhausted; our minds
    grow weary; our nerves are tensed beneath the
    strain.

If we try to face our temptations by ourselves,
    the fascination of the wrong things is too strong.
    Our resistance is defeated, and we do the things we
    know we should never do, because we cannot help
    it.

If we try to face our sorrows by ourselves,
    there is nothing to heal the wound upon our
    hearts, nothing to dry the fountain of our tears,
    nothing to comfort the loneliness which is more
    than we can bear.

If we try to face our problems by ourselves,
    we cannot see the right way; and, even when we
    see it, we cannot take it; and even when we take it,
    we cannot follow it to the end.

If we try to rid ourselves of faults by ourselves,
    we are forever defeated; the same sins conquer us;
    and we are never any farther on.

We know our need. Life has taught us that we cannot
walk alone. So be with us to help, to guide, to comfort,
to sustain, that in all the changes and the chances of
life, whatever light may shine or shadow fall, we may
meet life with steady eyes, and walk in wisdom and in

strength, in purity and in joy in the way everlasting, until we reach our journey's end; through Jesus Christ our Lord. Amen.[1]

*T*ake the Load Off

Exhausted. Weary. Wrung out. These are the words we hear from those who have been through the wringer of loss and grief. It's draining. Some days it's all we can do to get out of bed and get our shoes on.

We can be tired physically. We can be tired emotionally. We can be tired spiritually. It takes such an effort that the alternative of giving up and just existing seems so attractive.

Having a heavy heart drains the life right out of us. This is nothing new. We all struggle with this. Those who wrote Scripture struggled as well. Listen to their words:

> I am weary with my crying; my throat is parched, my eyes fail while I wait for my God (Psalm 69:3 NASB).

Is that a familiar feeling? We can be weary of wailing.

> He arose and struck the Philistines until his hand was weary and clung to the sword (2 Samuel 23:10 NASB).

We can become weary of struggling.

> I am weary with my sighing; every night I make my bed swim, I dissolve my couch with my tears. My eye

has wasted away with grief; it has become old because of my adversaries (Psalm 6:6-7 NASB).

When Jesus gives you a promise, it's not a prescription for something you take. He gives you himself.

> Come to me, all you who are weary and burdened, and I will give you rest. Take my yoke upon you and learn from me, for I am gentle and humble in heart, and you will find rest for your souls. For my yoke is easy and my burden is light (Matthew 11:28-30).

Sometimes our physical and emotional exhaustion comes because of scriptural exhaustion. It could be you've read the promises in Scripture again and again, but with no response you begin to doubt. Or, it could be your prayers just seem to bounce off the ceiling and go nowhere. We often get weary because we try to solve the problem ourselves, and then we have nothing left to give.

There's one person for you to talk to—and that's Jesus. The writer of Hebrews said, "Consider him...so that you will not grow weary and lose heart" (Hebrews 12:3).

Consider him...think about him...go to him...give him your load of cares.[1]

You're Not Alone in the Storm

Life is full of storms. You've been in them, so have I.

A number of years ago I went fishing on a lake in Minnesota with several relatives. It was a beautiful day. As the afternoon wore on, it became very calm and still. Suddenly my cousin said, "Let's head for shore…quick." I couldn't believe what I was hearing. The weather was great, and the fish were beginning to bite. But my cousin said, "Just wait." By the time we made the shoreline, ten minutes later, we were fighting 30- to 40-mile-an-hour winds. They seemed to come out of nowhere. For hours we huddled in our tents just waiting for them to be torn from their pegs.

Where did the storm come from? I wondered. One moment the sky was clear, the next we were being buffeted about by strong winds and a torrential rainstorm.

Storms are like that. They often appear out of nowhere at the "wrong time" and are totally inconvenient. They disrupt our plans and leave devastation in their path. Life is never the same after storms have swept through our lives.

There are other storms that do give us some warning. They appear gradually, and the weather forecasters are able to give us some indication in advance. To some degree, we can prepare for these if the predictions are consistent and accurate. But many times they aren't, and once again we find ourselves unprepared.

Storms come in all types, sizes, shapes, and intensities. There are rainstorms, firestorms, hailstorms, snowstorms, and windstorms. Nahum the prophet said, "[The Lord's] way is in the whirlwind and the storm" (Nahum 1:3).

I've been in some storms where the sky was split open by flashing, brilliant fingers of lightning followed by ear-deafening thunder. I've stood on the shoreline of Jackson Lake in the Grand Teton National Park and heard the thunder begin to roll through the Teton range 20 miles to the left of me and continue in front of me on up into Yellowstone National Park. It was a breathtaking, awesome experience.

Storms have a way of unsettling everything we thought was certain—especially the storms of life. Storms can rattle our beliefs as much as thunder rattles the windows. We want to be sure that we don't have to face the storms alone. We want someone with us, especially God.

There is a phrase in Scripture that is repeated over and over again. It's a reassuring and comforting phrase: "I will be with you."

God said this to Isaac, "Stay in this land for a while, and I will be with you and will bless you" (Genesis 26:3).

He said to Jacob, "Go back to the land of your fathers...and I will be with you" (Genesis 31:3).

He said to Joshua, "No one will be able to stand up against you all the days of your life. As I was with Moses, so I will be with you; I will never leave you nor forsake you" (Joshua 1:5).

God wants to assure us of the fact that he is always with us. There is a purpose in this phrase. "For everything that was written in the past was written to teach us, so that through endurance and the encouragement of the Scriptures we might have hope" (Romans 15:4). Hold on to these verses and remind yourself of God's promise, "I *will* be with you."

13

*H*e Is Working

I feel like an overused battery—depleted and drained. There's nothing more to give. My strength is gone. I can't take any more." Have you ever felt this way? Many have. We read the Scripture verse that says God won't give us more than we can bear; however, we feel that we've passed that point. Have you ever been there?

Often when we pray, we pray in very specific ways. We know three things: what we need, how we need it, and when we need it. When this happens, we become so focused on one particular need that it's difficult to see any other response coming from God. Other needs *are* being met, but these aren't registering because we're locked into one area of focus.

During the intensity of grief and loss, we have difficulty seeing how God is working in our lives because our pain limits our perception and understanding. This isn't a defect in us—it's our grief speaking.

When you're in grief or a crisis, don't expect yourself to understand all that is going on or the long-range purpose. That comes later. Then you will make discoveries that will amaze you. I've talked to many who said when they were in the midst of their crisis or grief they could neither praise God nor be thankful for anything he did. But afterward, they were able to see where he was present and working in their lives and realize the long-range results of their experience. One person said, "Somewhere during my darkest times I began to look for God and see him rather than any problems. I discovered his mercy and grace and how my life was changing in a way I never dreamed could be possible."

You may not be at this place yet. If not, you will need to accept this on faith—God is giving you gifts in this adversity that neither you nor I could receive in any other way. The greatest growth and change tends to come during our most difficult times. We all wish there was a different way.

In Philippians 3:10 we read, "[For my determined purpose is] that I may know Him [that I may progressively become more deeply and intimately acquainted with Him, perceiving and recognizing and understanding the wonders of His Person more strongly and more clearly], and that I may in the same way know the power outflowing from His resurrection [which it exerts over believers], and that I may so share His sufferings as to be continually transformed [in spirit into His likeness even] to His death, [in the hope]" (AMP). There is a joy in sharing the fellowship of Christ's sufferings. Out of this experience, your heart will probably be sensitized toward others in similar situations. Many people become more capable of extending compassion to others, but only after they've gone through similar losses and crises. Your experience is going to connect you to humanity in a new way. Our pain and suffering is a link to others. There will come a time when this *will* be evident, when it *will* make sense. Take comfort in that.[1]

14

ℋis Presence

When loss hits and grief is your existence, it's easy to feel stuck or even stagnant. That's not very comfortable. It's also easy to feel forgotten by others or think, "They're only calling because they feel obligated." You can even feel lonely in the presence of others. If your loss was a significant family member, the hole in your life is quite large. To fill this hole, some will sit and immerse themselves with memories, while others engage in frantic activity. When you're busy, you may not feel the pain as much or as deeply.

There is a simple phrase in the psalms that says "the help of His presence" (Psalm 42:5 NASB). There is a presence that can comfort if we're quiet enough to sense it. In the plan and purpose of God, provision has been made for you so you don't have to feel empty and you can feel secure. Sometimes it's difficult to think about teachings or doctrines when you're living in grief, but the truth of this phrase can bring the comfort you're seeking. You are a special person even if you don't feel like one. You've probably heard this many times, but we all need reminding:

> As Christians, we have been brought into a new and vital relationship with God the Father. We have been made members of his family. We are accepted by him and have access into his presence (Ephesians 1:3-6; Hebrews 4:16; 1 John 3:1-2; 4:16). We call him "Father." In a very real sense, therefore, we belong to him.

This relationship with God the Father serves as an antidote to feelings of anxiety or fear (1 John 4:16-18; 1 Peter 5:7; Proverbs 3:5-6).

A realization of our true value is derived from our relationship with Christ the Son (1 John 4:9). As we meditate on the price he paid for our redemption (1 Peter 1:18-19; Romans 5:6-8; Psalm 49:7-9) and realize that we have been made heirs of all the glories of his kingdom (Romans 8:16-17), we come to realize our true worth. It is quite apart from any work or service we might perform.

This relationship with the Lord Jesus Christ satisfactorily takes care of feelings of guilt (2 Corinthians 7:9-11) through confession (see 1 John 1:9), which leads to restoration.

Finally, our ability to cope with the harsh realities of life is restored as we allow God the Holy Spirit to control our lives (Ephesians 5:18). He indwells us and enables us to deal with each situation as it arises (John 14:16-17; 1 John 2:20). Through our relationship with him, we again experience a feeling of competence.

This relationship with the Holy Spirit satisfactorily takes care of feelings of anger (arising out of our frustration over things we cannot control or circumstances that cause us to feel rejected or humiliated).

Thus, your basic needs will be met as you establish or strengthen your union with each member of the Godhead.

While this may not solve all of your problems of loneliness, it will remove the sting of solitude so you will be able to face life with greater emotional stability.

It may be beneficial for you to read this over several times. Then look up the Bible references. Internalize the truths. Furthermore, constantly remind yourself of the truth of Psalm 34:

> I sought the LORD, and He answered me,
> And delivered me from all my fears.
> They looked to Him and were radiant,
> And their faces shall never be ashamed.
> This poor man cried and the LORD heard him
> And saved him out of all his troubles....
> The LORD is near to the brokenhearted,
> And saves those who are crushed in spirit
> (Psalm 34:4-6,18 NASB).

By developing a strong, internal God-consciousness, you can be strengthened to cope effectively with whatever lies before you.[1]

Why We Pray

Some who experience loss and grief stop praying altogether, while others intensify their prayers. Most of the prayers are requests. The emphasis is on "Help me change this situation! Intervene on my behalf!" Many ask, "What should I pray for? What would help me the most?" We make many requests of God. But prayer is more than requests. What you pray for is not the most important question—rather, it is why you pray. Praying is not really about us, it is about God. Who created us? Who loves us more than anyone? Who has redeemed us at a tremendous cost? Everything we have and are is from him. The purpose of prayer is to know him, not to get. C.S. Lewis said, "God designed the human machine to run on Himself. He Himself is the fuel our spirits were designed to burn, or the food our spirits were designed to feed on....God cannot give us happiness and peace apart from Himself, because it is not there. There is no such thing."[1]

Most of the time, in our prayers, we request actions or things. They don't satisfy. It's the relationship with God that's most important. The prayer "God, I want to know more of you" is a good beginning, especially when you feel alone and isolated in your grief. If you have lost a person, you probably ache for that person. And you miss him (her) not so much for what he could do for you, but for who he was. Your pain comes from the loss of a relationship. You long for him. We long for God and often aren't aware of it. As you pray and ask to know him more, read the Scriptures more. You will know him better, and your knowledge of him will increase. This happened to Job. Listen to him:

> I know that you can do all things,
>> no plan of yours can be thwarted....
>> Surely I spoke of things I did not understand,
>> things too wonderful for me to know....
>
> My ears had heard of you
>> but now my eyes have seen you.
>
> Therefore I despise myself
>> and repent in dust and ashes (Job 42:2-3,5-6).

Job encountered the living God in some kind of mystical experience. That much we know. The encounter stretched language and logic to the limit. Words failed him. Job became utterly still and silent, struck dumb by the unspeakable presence of God. He had no more questions, he made no more demands, he claimed no more rights. He simply bowed and surrendered because he had finally received what he most needed and longed for—an encounter with the living God.[2]

*Y*our Future

What you're experiencing right now will someday be a memory. It will be part of your history. Your future is being fashioned at this time. What will you say in the future about now?

In her book *When God Weeps*, Joni Eareckson Tada talks about her experience:

> Time is slippery stuff. The past always looks different than it did back when. Memory is selective. It chooses only a few highlights of lasting importance from all that happened. When we recall pain in the past, we do so with a perspective we simply didn't have when going through it. We didn't understand how it would all pan out. In the middle of suffering we see only confusion. For me it was a bizarre mix of tie-dyed T-shirts, the smell of pot in the hallways of the state institution, and thoughts of suicide.
>
> If we were looking for roads that led somewhere through the pain, we were doing just that—looking, not finding them. Later, it's different. In my case, thirty years later, I'm finally understanding. I have found the path. All because I see things differently.
>
> It depends on our perspective—where in time we are looking from. When looking back on heartache, the pain fades like a hazy memory. The trauma has

dulled like an old photograph. Only the results survive, the things of lasting importance—like the good marriage, the successful career, or in my case, the acceptance of a wheelchair. These are the events that rise and remain, like stepping-stones above raging waters. These are the things that carry us to the other side of suffering, to the present—the place where we have a sense of "arrival," the place where we are more "us" than we were years earlier.

When we come "through the valley of the shadow of death," we are different people. Better, stronger, and wiser. It's what happens on the other side. He "prepares a table before me in the presence of my enemies"; like me wheeling placidly by a faded poster of a huge marijuana leaf. He "anoints my head with oil; my cup overflows" with the satisfaction of surviving suffering with a smile (Psalm 23:4-5).

The Bible constantly tries to get us to look at life this way. It steadfastly tries to implant the perspective of the future into our present. It is like a voice counseling us, "This is the way it's all going to turn out, this is how it will all seem when it's over, a better way, I promise." It's a view that separates what is lasting from what will fall by the wayside.

Scripture can do no less. It only deals in realities, always underscoring the final results—the heart settled, the soul rejoicing. And so Scripture urges: "Consider it pure joy, my brothers, whenever you face trials of many kinds" (James 1:2). It reminds us:

> "It was good for me to be afflicted so that I might learn your decrees" (Psalm 119:71).

> "For our light and momentary troubles are achieving for us an eternal glory that far outweighs them all" (2 Corinthians 4:17).

"Not only so, but we also rejoice in our sufferings" (Romans 5:3).

"'For I know the plans I have for you,' declares the Lord, 'plans to prosper you and not to harm you, plans to give you hope and a future'" (Jeremiah 29:11).

"Blessed [happy] is the man you discipline, O LORD, the man you teach from your law; you grant him relief from days of trouble" (Psalm 94:12-13).

The Bible blatantly tells us to "rejoice in suffering" and "welcome trials as friends" because God wants us to step into the reality he has in mind for us, the only reality that ultimately counts. It requires gutsy faith to do so, but as we trust God, we move beyond the present into the future. In fact, we enter the very future God intends for us. "Your new life, which is your *real* life—even though invisible to spectators—is with Christ in God. *He* is your life. When Christ (your real life, remember) shows up again on this earth, you'll show up, too—the real you, the glorious you" (Colossians 3:3 MSG).[1]

17

$\mathcal{G}$rief Changes You

Questions are a part of grief. Grief is such a new venture for most that we end up feeling our way. The worst questions are those we don't ask and attempt to answer ourselves. One of the most common questions is, "How long does it take to recover from a loss?" There are many variables to this question, such as, "What was the loss?" "How close were you?" and "How much investment did you have with what or whom you lost?"

If your loss was a death, it will take as long as it takes. No one can really tell you how long. Was it a parent, a sibling, a spouse, a close friend, or a child? Some friendships are closer relationships than a relative. And if your loss was your child, you have experienced what is called the ultimate bereavement or the worst loss. When a child dies, parents carry with them a shadow grief. It can be triggered by expected and unexpected events for the rest of their lives.

Sometimes we spend months or even years grieving in advance of the death if it's a terminal illness.

One of the indications of grief being completed is when we're able to think of the one we lost without pain. We will tend to have a sense of sadness when we think of the person we loved, but it's not that overwhelming and devastating sadness we used to have.

Carol Fredericks Ebeling offers four "mile markers" that help grievers determine their progress toward integrating the loss:

1. The griever uses the hard words for death. Rather than use euphemisms such as "My child is gone," they say straightforwardly, "My child died."

2. The griever talks about the loss without being overwhelmed by tears.

3. The griever can feel good about feeling good.

4. The griever can risk change. Statements such as "He wouldn't want me to…" or "She would want to…" do not bring the grief.

Your answer is also based on your response to three questions:

What have I lost?

How do I feel about it?

Who am I now without…?[1]

If it hasn't happened already, this will. Friends will say to you, "You should be over your grief by now." Remember, they are not experts. It's all right to say, "No, I shouldn't. This is not a journey of weeks or months, but years. And when you see me upset, that's all right because I'm not broken, I don't need to be fixed. Just be there for me."

Remember this: Grief reannounces itself around anniversaries, holidays, and special days.

Also remember in grief there is no "normal." You won't get back to normal. But if you cooperate with your grief, sometimes a new "normal" develops.

You will be involved in "grief work," which simply means paying close attention to grief. It's the energy you need to exert to take this loss and integrate it into the story of your life. Grief work is *not* about getting over it and moving on with your life. You don't do "something *about* your grief, but do something *with* it."[2]

A final thought: "In grief, your journey will never end. People do not 'get over' grief....We are forever changed by the experiences of grief."[3]

Despair or Praise?

Despair is not a pleasant experience. The word itself is not very pretty. It means an utter loss of hope. There's such finality to it. Perhaps you've been there or this is where you're living now. It could be that we all have at one time or another. David, who wrote so many psalms, was no stranger to despair. He felt it. Trials were part of his life, just like they're part of ours. And when they happen, don't be surprised by their presence—we were forewarned. Peter said, "Beloved, do not think it strange concerning the fiery trial which is to try you, as though some strange thing happened to you" (1 Peter 4:12 NKJV).

The Message translation puts it in a unique way: "Friends, when life gets really difficult, don't jump to the conclusion that God isn't on the job. Instead, be glad that you are in the very thick of what Christ experienced. This is a spiritual refining process, with glory just around the corner" (1 Peter 4:12).

In Psalm 71, David shares his despair as well as his trust in God. In his cry to God he said, "Deliver me in your righteousness and cause me to escape." He wanted out of all the problems he was experiencing. In many ways, we too, would like out of the pain of our loss. When a crisis or loss hits, we wish we could hit the rewind button and go back to the way things were. Our response of "I'd like to go to sleep and wake up and find it was just a bad dream," is the same thing. Later David said, "Deliver me, O my God, out of the hand of the wicked, out of the hand of the unrighteous and cruel man. For You are my hope, O Lord GOD, You are my trust from my youth. By You I have been upheld from birth; You are He who took me out of my mother's womb. My praise shall be continually of You" (Psalm 71:4-6 NKJV).

What David did at this time was remember—He remembered how God had been faithful over the years. Can you remember those times? How was God faithful to you five years ago? ten years ago? fifteen years ago?

David was honest. He was blunt. He voiced his pain. And then in the midst of it, his prayer is filled with worship and praise. Listen to his words. Look at the rest of the psalm:

- My praise shall be continually of You (verse 6).

- Let my mouth be filled with Your praise and with Your glory all the day (verse 8).

- But I will hope continually and will praise You yet more and more. My mouth shall tell of Your righteousness and Your salvation all the day, for I do not know their limits (verses 14-15).

- Also with the lute I will praise You—and Your faithfulness, O my God! To You I will sing with the harp, O Holy One of Israel. My lips shall greatly rejoice when I sing to You, and my soul, which You have redeemed. My tongue also shall talk of Your righteousness all the day long; for they are confounded, for they are brought to shame who seek my hurt (verses 22-24).

Perhaps you're praising God already. Or it may take months to arrive at this place. It happened with David. Expect it to occur. Wait. Pray. Read God's Word. In Psalm 71, cynicism is replaced by faith.[1]

$\mathcal{H}$e Knows Your Name

$\mathcal{T}$ommy Walker's song *He Knows My Name* has ministered to many. Some of the words are:

> I have a Father,
> He calls me His own.
> He'll never leave me
> No matter where I go.
>
> He knows my name,
> He knows my every thought.
> He sees each tear that falls
> And hears me when I call.[1]

Many of us have experienced a comfort and peace we couldn't explain while enduring the most traumatic of circumstances. That's because the God we worship isn't just the God of truths, facts, and numbers. He is also the God of compassion, kindness, and comfort. In fact, he calls himself the Wonderful Counselor and Prince of Peace (see Isaiah 9:6).

Why people roll up their sleeves and try to endure such tragedies by their own strength is something I'll never know. Psalm 46:1 says that God is available to be our "ever-present help in [times of] trouble." Jesus did in fact tell us that "in the world ye shall have tribulation," but he went on with the promise, saying we could "be of good cheer, I have overcome the world" (John 16:33 KJV).

Though we may not totally grasp the depth of meaning of this verse, we do know a couple of things that Jesus is definitely saying here. First, Jesus is releasing and encouraging us to be joyful even when we find ourselves in the midst of life's challenging struggles and tragedies. During these times, we can still, by his grace and indwelling Holy Spirit, be cheerful—even to the point of rejoicing! This is an important way we can express our faith. It also helps defeat the strategies of our enemy (the devil), our weak flesh, and the pull toward discouragement and fear.

Certainly there are times to mourn. Jesus not only acknowledges those times when he says, "Blessed are they that mourn" (Matthew 5:4 KJV), but he also instructs us to empathize with others—to "mourn with those who mourn" (Romans 12:15). In this way, we comfort others as we ourselves have been comforted.

The second thing Jesus is saying in this verse is that we will live in eternity and our earthly life is not the end of the story. In fact, life on Earth is just a blip on a radar screen—less than a microsecond of time in our true lifespan—if we have accepted and taken hold of God's incredibly generous offer of salvation through Jesus Christ. When we take this eternal perspective, we also find great comfort because we know our God will make things right on that great day when Jesus returns and reigns in the new heaven and new earth. Our comfort is further secured in knowing that he removes all our sorrows, heals all our wounds, and wipes away all our tears.

Sometimes the greatest comfort comes in knowing that this world is not our home. Jesus will come for us one day. "Amen. Come, Lord Jesus" (Revelation 22:20).

$\mathcal{T}$ell God

$\sim$

$\mathbf{I}$f you had an audience with God today and could ask or say anything to him that you wanted to—I mean *really* wanted to—what would you ask? Would you be as bold as Job? Job challenged God because he was silent. Job had experienced losses and was overcome with grief. He also had to tolerate three friends who tormented and wounded him with their words.

> My complaint is still bitter today. I groan because God's heavy hand is on me. I wish I knew where to find God so I could go to where he lives. I would present my case before him and fill my mouth with arguments....If I go to the east, God is not there; if I go to the west, I do not see him. When he is at work in the north, I catch no sight of him; when he turns to the south, I cannot see him. But God knows the way that I take, and when he has tested me, I will come out like gold (Job 23:2-4,8-9 NCV).

After reading this passage, one man said, "One bold message in the Book of Job is that you can say anything to God. Throw at him your grief, your anger, your doubt, your bitterness, your betrayal, your disappointment—he can absorb them all. As often as not, spiritual giants of the Bible are shown contending with God. They prefer to go away limping, like Jacob, rather than to shut God out.

In this respect, the Bible prefigures a tenet of modern psychology: You can't deny your feelings or make them disappear, so you might as well express them. God can deal with every human response save one. He cannot abide the response I fall back on instinctively; an attempt to ignore him or treat him as though he does not exist. That response never once occurred to Job."[1]

Others have expressed their honest concern to God. Perhaps this echoes your thoughts and feelings.

> God, where are you?…
> Speak to me! Teach me!
> Rebuke me! Strike me down!
> But do not remain silent.
> The God who is mute. Is that who you are?
> You have revealed yourself as the speaking God—
>   our communicating Cosmos.
> You pointed Abraham to a city whose builder
>   and maker was God.
> You revealed your divine name to Moses.
> You spoke with clarity
> to David, to Ruth, to Esther,
> to Isaiah, to Ezekiel, to Daniel,
> to Mary, to Paul, and a host of others.
> Why are the heavens made of iron for me?
> Job, I know, experienced you as the hidden God.
> And Elijah held a lonely vigil over earthquake, wind,
>   and fire. Me, too.
> O God of wonder and mystery, teach me by means of
>   your
> Wondrous, terrible, loving, all-embracing silence.
> Amen.[2]

What do you need to express to God? Even if you don't hear back, he hears you. And by the way, you do have an audience with God—at any time.

21

The Sea of Discouragement

The bottom dropped out of my life. I feel shipwrecked. I am so discouraged." For some, disappointment comes and goes, while for others it's a lifestyle. Where does it come from? It emerges when our plans don't work out. It happens when others don't reach out to help as we need them to. Discouragement has been described as a dry barren wind off a blistering desert, and it causes us to wilt. On other occasions, it's like a chilling mist that numbs our thoughts and fogs the road ahead of us. Discouragement can take the heart right out of you.

Have you been there? It's part of life, though we might wish otherwise. Perhaps you, like many others, have made the statement, "I'm *so* discouraged." People describe discouragement in various ways:

- "It took the wind right out of my sails."
- "It felt like I was knocked right off my feet."
- "It sucked my drive and energy right out of me."
- "It was a form of paralysis. Physically I could move; but in another sense I couldn't.
- "The daylight looked dark even though the sun was out."

So what is this malady called discouragement? Let's look at the word and take it apart.

You find the word *courage*, with its root syllable *cor*. This is the Latin word for *heart*, which is the center of this condition. *Discouragement* is literally the loss of heart. When discouragement enters into our lives, hope exits. When discouragement gains a foothold, we are tempted to give up. The psalmist felt this way: "Come, Lord, and show me your mercy, for I am helpless, overwhelmed, in deep distress; my problems go from bad to worse. Oh, save me from them all" (Psalm 25:16-17 TLB).

What about discouragement caused by adversity? That can be a major cause. What can you do? Paul learned how to deal with adversity. "We are hard pressed on every side, but not crushed; perplexed, but not in despair; persecuted, but not abandoned; struck down, but not destroyed" (2 Corinthians 4:8-9). Paul also said, "Therefore we do not lose heart. Though outwardly we are wasting away, yet inwardly we are being renewed day by day. For our light and momentary troubles are achieving for us an eternal glory that far outweighs them all" (2 Corinthians 4:16-17).

Fresh strength is what every discouraged person needs. Where do you get your strength? God. He is the true source of strength. The phrase to remember in the midst of discouragement is God's words to Joshua, "Be strong and courageous." God continues, "Do not be terrified; do not be discouraged, for the LORD your God will be with you wherever you go" (Joshua 1:9). God *is* the source of our strength.

Eventually, we come to the place where we're able to say, "This makes us confident. No matter what happens." This is an attitude, a personal choice. Do you know what the word *attitude* means? Attitude is a manner of acting, thinking, or feeling that shows one's disposition, opinion, or mental set.

This attitude of confidence has worked for many who faced and lived with physical adversity. It worked for John Milton, who was blind. He wrote *Paradise Lost* and *Paradise Regained*. It also worked for Beethoven, who, in spite of his deafness, gave us the Ninth Symphony. It worked for John Bunyan, who wrote *Pilgrim's Progress* while in prison. And remember Helen Keller, who was deaf and blind? She said, "Neither darkness nor silence can impede the progress of the human spirit."

Is it possible to regain courage even when you are discouraged? Yes. Scripture contains many messages about fighting discouragement. See how these folks battled it.

This is the message of Job, who had virtually lost everything but his life: "Though he slay me, yet will I hope in him; I will surely defend my ways to his face" (Job 13:15).

This is the message of David: "Even though I walk through the valley of the shadow of death, I will fear no evil, for you are with me; your rod and your staff, they comfort me" (Psalm 23:4).

This is the message of Isaiah: "You will keep in perfect peace him whose mind is steadfast, because he trusts in you" (Isaiah 26:3).

This is the message of Paul: "For I am convinced that neither death nor life, neither angels nor demons, neither the present nor the future, nor any powers, neither height nor depth, nor anything else in all creation, will be able to separate us from the love of God that is in Christ Jesus our Lord" (Romans 8:38-39).

Read these verses daily if you're struggling with discouragement.

22

What Do You Remember?

If your loss was a loved one, what do you think about during the day? Memories are an important part of our lives. Often your thoughts are dominated by the one you lost. You see his (her) face, hear his voice, smell his fragrance. And you think, "It wasn't long enough. He wasn't with me long enough." Well, most of us feel that way. It's never enough. It's never convenient. It's never the "right" time. There's always this void a person leaves. But we need to remember that even though we focus on segments of time, God has a different perspective and sees time differently. God looks more at a person's fulfillment of his purpose in life rather than how long he or she has been on this earth. Have you looked at that perspective rather than at time?

Many people also get stuck thinking about the lost hours or days or weeks of their lives, especially if this was a difficult or painful time. We call these the dark or down times. Zig Zigler, in his *Confessions of a Grieving Christian,* said:

> If we concentrate solely on a loved one's pain and suffering, the physical appearance as a result of an accident or wasting disease, or the loss of function, we will continue to live in a nightmare of gruesome and

sad memories. It is wiser and grief-relieving to put this period of the person's life into the perspective of his entire life. Although this season might have lasted for days, weeks, months, or even years, it was only a *season* of his life. I encourage you to bring up memories that are from seasons in which the loved one's health, appearance, mental state, and emotional state were good, even superior! Recall the person when he lived with vitality, energy, laughter, loving actions toward others, and ongoing praise and worship of the Lord. Concentrate on the good times, the family jokes and moments of merriment, and the sweet memories of times spent together. Choose to be encouraged that most of the seasons of a loved one's life were very likely good seasons.

And if your loved one never experienced any of the above, take comfort in the fact that he now has a glorified body and will enjoy perfect health, total peace, and absolute joy throughout eternity. All that the loved one experienced in this life was experienced in only a fleeting moment against the unending panorama of heaven. Against the length of eternity, our time spent on this earth cannot even be mathematically calculated. This forever season of a loved one's life so far overshadows even his best seasons of life on earth that they cannot be compared.

If our departed ones could come back to us and tell us about their experience with the Lord in heaven, I feel certain they would tell us three things. First, they would tell us to concentrate on the way they were when they were at their best in this life. Second, they would tell us to enjoy our lives to the fullest and choose to fill them with the best memories and experiences possible. Third, they would tell us to spend more time getting to know Christ better.

This approach is not denying the reality or even the benefit of grief, but it is putting the focus on a person's whole life. While we can do nothing to bring back a loved one, we can bring to our minds and hearts the fond memories of happy occasions so that we can continue to produce more such memories of ourselves and our other loved ones who still walk this earth with us.[1]

And so today, what else can you remember? You'll be surprised at the comfort this can bring.

23

You're Not Going Crazy

I'm past the point of going
quietly insane.
I'm getting quite
noisy about it.
The neighbors must think
I'm mad.
The neighbors, for once,
think right.

—Peter McWilliams
How to Survive the Loss of a Love

A strange poem, but perhaps not. The feelings of grief feel a bit crazy. As a counselor, the following list is what I share with others who have experienced a major loss and usually their response is, "Yes, that's me":

- distorted thinking patterns, "crazy" and/or irrational thoughts, fearful thoughts

- feelings of despair and hopelessness

- out of control or numbed emotions

- changes in sensory perceptions (sight, taste, smell, etc.)

- memory lags and mental "short-circuits"

- inability to concentrate

- obsessive focus on the loved one

- losing track of time

- increase or decrease of appetite and/or sexual desire

- difficulty falling or staying asleep

- dreams in which the deceased seems to visit the griever

- nightmares in which death themes are repeated

- physical illness like the flu, headaches, or other maladies

- shattered beliefs about life, the world, and even God[1]

It is not unusual for people to report that they feel as if they are "going crazy" following a major loss. When they describe the symptoms of their "craziness," it becomes apparent they are describing the symptoms of intense stress and anxiety.

Many people report short-term memory loss. The mind is paralyzed and overloaded. Loss of memory is annoying, but it will pass. It will pass far more quickly if you go easy on yourself and accept this as a temporary response to your grief.

If you lost someone close to you, people also report a reliving of the last time they saw their loved ones alive. Your mind occasionally flashes back to your last visit with him (her). That memory can be so vivid, you almost feel as if you're there.

Others report a loss of concentration. Their racing thoughts swirl in their minds in no pattern and to no purpose. They can't think anything through to a conclusion. On the other hand, some report a slowing of their thoughts, or a kind of clouded consciousness, as if they are moving through a mist. They can't focus;

nothing seems quite real. All of these symptoms are perfectly ordinary considering the intensity of the sorrow being endured.

Still others tell about symptoms that would suggest panic attacks, a fight-or-flight response: increased heart rate, speeding of respiration, cotton mouth, profuse perspiring. Unlike panic attacks, however, these symptoms are brought on by an identifiable event and are likely to disappear as people move through their grief.

Some develop physical symptoms that mimic other ailments. For example, people may believe they are having a heart attack, with all the attendant symptoms, or get migraines, or they develop the habit of grinding their teeth.

Still others seem as if they have become depressed. And although the symptoms of depression—intense sadness, feelings of helplessness, hopelessness, and powerlessness—are the same as many of the symptoms of grief, there is a difference. Grief is a natural process that comes to an end without intervention. Depression generally requires professional intervention in order to alleviate it. Depression may develop if a person tries to bypass the grieving process, but the process itself is not depression.

If you have found yourself experiencing any of these symptoms, take heart. They will pass. Naturally, it is wise to have a doctor look into any alarming physical symptoms, but chances are those symptoms will disappear in time—if you are faithful about processing your grief.

The symptoms we manifest during this time of crisis are actually a sign of the wondrous way God created human beings. Our minds and bodies are designed to declare a sort of "red alert" that is meant to force us to slow down and pay attention to our needs.

So, if possible, be grateful for the way God has provided for every eventuality in your life and try to slow down. Remember, go easy on yourself. This too shall pass. You're normal.[2]

24

Why Grief?

When you enter into grief, you enter into the valley of shadows. There is nothing heroic or noble about grief. It is painful. It is work. It is a lingering process. But it is a necessary process for all types of losses. It has been labeled everything from intense mental anguish to acute sorrow to deep remorse.

The many emotions involved in the grief process can seem out of control and often appear in conflict with one another. With each loss comes bitterness, emptiness, apathy, love, anger, guilt, sadness, fear, self-pity, and helplessness. These feelings have been described in this way:

> These feelings usher in the emotional freeze that covers solid ground with ice, making movement in any direction seem precarious and dangerous. Growth is hidden, progress seems blocked, and one bleakly speculates that just because the crocuses made it through the snow last year is no reason to believe they can do it again this year. It's not a pretty picture.[1]

Does God understand our pain and our grief? In the early portion of Genesis we find the answer. Genesis 6:6 says, "He was grieved in His heart" (NASB). God knows grief.

When grief is your companion, you experience it psychologically through your feelings, thoughts, and attitudes. It impacts

you socially as you interact with others. You experience it physically as it affects your health and is expressed in bodily symptoms.

Grief encompasses a number of changes. It appears differently
at various times, and it flits in and out of your life. It is a natural,
normal, predictable, and expected reaction. It is not an abnormal
response. In fact, just the opposite is true. The absence of grief is
abnormal. Grief is your own personal experience. Your loss does
not have to be accepted or validated by others for you to experience and express grief.[2]

Why do we have to go through this experience? What is the
purpose? Grief responses express basically three things:

- Through grief you express your feelings about your loss.

- Through grief you express your protest at the loss, as well as
  your desire to change what happened and have it not be
  true.

- Through grief you express the effects you have experienced
  from the devastating impact of the loss.[3]

The purpose of grieving over your loss is to get beyond these
reactions, to face your loss, and work on adapting to it. The over-
all purpose of grief is to bring you to the point of making necessary changes so you can live with the loss in a healthy way. Your
eventual goal is to be able to say:

> *This loss I've experienced is a crucial upset in my life. In
> fact, it is the worst thing that will ever happen to me. But
> is it the end of my life? No. I can still have a rich and ful-
> filling life. Grief has been my companion and has taught
> me much. I can use it to grow into a stronger person than
> I was before my loss.*[4]

Mourning is the necessary process of returning back to life after we have been jolted from its road. It involves leaving behind what needs to be left behind, bringing along what needs to be brought along, and learning to distinguish between the two.[5]

$\mathcal{I}$t's Called
"The Gift of Grace"

Our belief in God and how we perceive God—our theology—will affect how we cope with a loss or a crisis. Our lives are based upon our theology; however, many are frightened by it.

Often when we go through difficult losses and crises we are forced to reevaluate what we truly believe. Unfortunately, many determine what they believe by what they are going through. They allow their theology to be determined by their circumstances. When they hit the problems of life, they seem to negate the promises of God and begin to wonder if he cares!

Sometimes a crisis changes our view of God. Author Max Lucado describes the process well:

> There is a window in your heart through which you can see God. Once upon a time that window was clear. Your view of God was crisp. You could see God as vividly as you could see a gentle valley or hillside. The glass was clean, the pane unbroken.
>
> You knew God. You knew how he worked. You knew what he wanted you to do. No surprises. Nothing unexpected. You knew that God had a will, and you continually discovered what it was.

Then, suddenly, the window cracked. A pebble broke the window. A pebble of pain.

Perhaps that stone struck when you were a child and a parent left home—forever. Maybe the rock hit in adolescence when your heart was broken. Maybe you made it into adulthood before the window was cracked. But then the pebble came.

Was it a phone call? "We have your daughter at the station, you'd better come down."

Was it a letter on the kitchen table? "I've left. Don't try to reach me. Don't try to call me. It's over. I just don't love you any more."

Was it a diagnosis from the doctor? "I'm afraid our news is not very good."

Was it a telegram? "We regret to inform you that your son is missing in action."[1]

Why do we end up feeling disappointed by God? Is it really because of him, or could it be because of our own expectations? We have our own unexpressed agenda. We believe, "If God is God, then…" But does our agenda match the teaching of Scripture? Those who believe in the sovereignty and caring nature of a loving God have a better basis upon which to approach life—and to deal with crisis.

A book that has spoken to me every time I've read it is Lewis Smedes' *How Can It Be All Right When Everything Is All Wrong?* He has been through life's tough times. His insights and sensitivity to life's crises and God's presence and involvement in our lives can answer many of our questions. One of his personal experiences describes how our faith helps us move through life's changes:

The other night, trying to sleep, I amused myself by trying to recall the most happy moments of my life. I let my mind skip and dance where it was led. I thought of leaping down from a rafter in a barn, down into a deep loft of sweet, newly mown hay. That was a superbly happy moment. But somehow my mind was also seduced to a scene some years ago that, as I recall it, must have been the most painful of my life. Our firstborn child was torn from our hands by what felt to me like a capricious deity I did not want to call God. I felt ripped off by a cosmic con-artist. And for a little while, I thought I might not easily ever smile again.

But then, I do not know how, in some miraculous shift in my perspective, a strange and inexpressible sense came to me that my life, our lives were still good, that it is good because it is *given*, and that its possibilities were still incalculable. Down into the gaps of feeling left over from the pain came a sense of givenness that nothing explains. It can only be felt as a gift of grace. An irrepressible impulse of blessing came from my heart to God for his sweet gift. And that was joy…in spite of pain. Looking back, it seems to me now that I have never again known so sharp, so severe, so saving a sense of gratitude and so deep a joy, or so honest.[2]

Have you experienced the gift of grace yet? If not, it's definitely in your future.

26

*G*od's Timetable

What God allows us to experience is for our growth. God has arranged the seasons of nature to produce growth, and he arranges the experiences of the seasons of our lives for growth also. Some days bring sunshine and some bring storms. Both are necessary. He knows the amount of pressure we can handle. First Corinthians 10:13 tells us he will "...not let you be tempted beyond what you can bear." But he does let us be tempted, feel pain, and experience suffering. He does not always give us what we think we need or want, but what will promote growth.

When we have suffered a loss, we feel like the disciples adrift in that small boat during the storm on the Sea of Galilee. The waves throw us about, and just as we get our legs under us, we're hit from another direction. They struggled on the Sea of Galilee, and we struggle on the sea of life. All of us are afraid of capsizing. All we see are waves that seem to grow larger each moment. We're afraid. However, Jesus came to the disciples, and he comes to us today with the same message: "It is I; don't be afraid" (John 6:20).

We ask God, "Where are you?" but he is always there in the midst of the crisis. We ask him, "When? When will you answer?" As the psalmist cried, "How long, O LORD, will you forget me forever? How long will you hide your face from me? How long must I wrestle with my thoughts and every day have sorrow in my heart? How long will my enemy triumph over me?" (Psalm 13:1-2). We want God to act according to our timetable, but the Scriptures say, "Be still before the LORD and wait patiently for him" (Psalm 37:7). We become restless in waiting, and to block out the pain of waiting, we are often driven to frantic activity. This does not help, but resting before the Lord does.

> Often waiting is a time of darkening clouds. Our skies do not lighten. Instead, everything seems to become even more grim.
>
> Yet the darkening of our skies may forecast the dawn. It is in the gathering folds of deepening shadows that God's hidden work for us takes place. The present, no matter how painful, is of utmost importance.
>
> Somewhere, where our eyes cannot see and our ears are unable to hear, God is. And God is at work.[1]

You may not feel that God is doing anything to help you recover. Why? Because we want recovery *now*. The instant-solution philosophy of our society often invades a proper perspective of God. We complain about waiting a few weeks or days, but to God a day is as a thousand years and a thousand years an instant. God works in hidden ways, even when you and I are totally frustrated by his apparent lack of response. We are merely unaware that he is active. Hear the words of Isaiah for people then and now:

> Since ancient times no one has heard,
>   no ear has perceived,
> no eyes have seen any God besides you,
>   who acts on behalf of those who wait for him.
> You come to the help of those who gladly do right,
>   who remember your ways (Isaiah 64:4-5).

God has a reason for everything he does and a schedule for when he does it:

" 'For I know the plans I have for you,' declares the LORD, 'plans to prosper you and not to harm you, plans to give you hope and a future'" (Jeremiah 29:11). Give yourself permission not to know what, not to know how, and not to know when. Even though you feel adrift on the turbulent ocean, God is holding you and knows the direction of your drift. Giving yourself permission to wait can give you hope. It is all right for God to ask us to wait weeks and months and even years. During that time when we do not receive the answer and/or solution we think we need, he gives us his presence: "But I trust in you, O LORD; I say, 'You are my God.' My times are in your hands" (Psalm 31:14-15).

27

The Applause of Heaven

In Max Lucado's inspirational book *The Applause of Heaven*, he ends with a chapter on going home. He begins the chapter by describing his conclusion to a long trip and finally arriving at the airport. His wife and three daughters are excited that he is home. But one of them has a very interesting response. In the midst of the shouts of joy that he is home, she stops long enough to clap. She applauds for him. Isn't that different? But isn't it affirming and appropriate! Then he proceeds to talk about the Christian's ultimate home and homegoing. Surely Jesus, too, will clap when we arrive home.

In Revelation 21:1-4, we read John's description of what our homegoing will be like:

> Then I saw a new heaven and a new earth, for the first heaven and the first earth had passed away, and there was no longer any sea. I saw the Holy City, the new Jerusalem, coming down out of heaven from God, prepared as a bride beautifully dressed for her husband. And I heard a loud voice from the throne saying, "Now the dwelling of God is with men, and he will live with them. They will be his people, and God himself will be with them and be their God. He will wipe every tear from their eyes. There will be no more death or

mourning or crying or pain, for the old order of things has passed away.

John says that someday God will wipe away your tears. The same hands that stretched the heavens will touch your cheeks. The same hands that formed the mountains will caress your face. The same hands that curled in agony as the Roman spike cut through will someday cup your face and brush away your tears forever.

When you think of a world where there will be no reason to cry, ever, doesn't it make you want to go home?

"There will be no more death…" John declares. Can you imagine it? A world with no hearses or morgues or cemeteries or tombstones? Can you imagine a world with no spades of dirt thrown on caskets? No names chiseled into marble? No funerals? No black dresses? No black wreaths?

In the next world, John says, "goodbye" will never be spoken.[1]

Every person on earth is appointed to die at some time. We fear it, resist it, try to postpone it, and even deny its existence. But it won't work. We cannot keep our loved ones from dying. We cannot keep ourselves from dying. But we can see it from God's perspective. Max Lucado concludes his book with what homecoming means from a new perspective:

> Before you know it, your appointed arrival time will come; you'll descend the ramp and enter the City. You'll see faces that are waiting for you. You'll hear your name spoken by those you love. And, maybe, just maybe—in the back, behind the crowds—the One who would rather die than live without you will remove his pierced hands from his heavenly robe and…*applaud*.[2]

Yes, your loved ones who died are now saying "hello" in heaven. Isn't that a comforting thought?

28

The Questions
of Grief

Some days in grief you don't think in statements, but more in questions, which run through your mind like a continuous carousel. Around and around they go, searching for answers, but none will satisfy. Have you had those days in which the questions are present and the answers are not? You're not alone. Listen to Job's questions:

> Why was I not stillborn? Why did I not give up the ghost when my mother bore me? (Job 3:11 AMP).

> Is there not an [appointed] warfare *and* hard labor to man upon earth? And are not his days like the days of a hireling? (Job 7:1 AMP).

> Why do You hide Your face [as if offended], and alienate me as if I were Your enemy? (Job 13:24 AMP).

> Where then is my hope? And, if I have hope, who will see [its fulfillment]? (Job 17:15 AMP).

Who was he asking? God. And God's answer? Silence. Did you even consider the possibility that the best answer at times is silence? When there are no real answers or the answers are not

71

what you want to hear or you're not at a place where you can receive them, take comfort in the silence.

Rainer Maria Rilke helps us respond to questions:

> Be patient towards all that is unsolved in your heart and try to see the questions themselves like locked rooms and like books that are written in a very foreign tongue. Do not now seek the answers, which cannot be given to you because you would not be able to live them. And the point is, live everything. Live the questions now. Perhaps you will then gradually, without noticing it, live along some distant day into the answers.[1]

It helps to share your questions with others, but before doing so, let them know you're not looking for answers. You just wanted them to know what is occurring within your heart and mind.

Don't be afraid of your questions and their boldness. God knows our thoughts and what we will say before we ever say it, so talk to him.

Hear the prayer of this honest person:

> How shall I pray?
> Are tears prayers, Lord?
> Are screams prayers,
> or groans
> or sighs
> or curses?
> Can trembling hands be lifted to you,
> or clenched fists
> or the cold sweat that trickles down my back
> or the cramps that knot my stomach?
> Will you accept my prayers, Lord,
> my real prayers,
> rooted in the muck and mud and rock of my life,

and not just my pretty, cut-flower, gracefully arranged
bouquet of words?
Will you accept me, Lord,
as I really am,
a messed up mixture of glory and grime?[2]

May the God of all comfort be with you in your searching.

reams

Have you ever heard God speak? Many have. Oh, perhaps not in an audible voice, but he speaks in other ways. Here are some insights from Job:

> Indeed God speaks….In a dream, a vision of the night, when the sound sleep falls on men. While they slumber in their beds, then He opens the ears of men, and seals their instruction" (Job 33:14-16 NASB).

Frederick Buechner said:

> Every once in a while, if you're like me, you have a dream that wakes you up. Sometimes it's a bad dream—a dream in which the shadows become so menacing that your heart skips a beat and you come awake to the knowledge that not even the actual darkness of night is as fearsome as the dreamed darkness, not even the shadows without as formidable as the shadows within. Sometimes it's a sad dream—a dream sad enough to bring real tears to your sleeping eyes so that it's your tears that you wake up by, wake up to. Or again, if you're like me, there are dreams that take a turn so absurd that you wake up laughing—as if you need to be awake to savor the full richness of the comedy. Rarest

of all is the dream that wakes you with what I can only call its truth.

The path of your dream winds now this way, now that—one scene fades into another, people come and go the way they do in dreams—and then suddenly, deep out of wherever it is that dreams come from, something rises up that shakes you into the foundations. The mystery of the dream suddenly lifts like fog and for an instant you glimpse a truth truer than any you knew if only a truth about yourself. It is too much truth for the dream to hold anyway; and the dream breaks.[1]

If you're experiencing difficulty sleeping, try this prayer before bed:

Dear God,

We give thanks for the darkness of the night where lies the world of dreams. Guide us closer to our dreams so that we may be nourished by them. Give us good dreams and memory of them so that we may carry their poetry and mystery into our daily lives.

Grant us deep and restful sleep that we may wake refreshed with strength enough to renew a world grown tired.

We give thanks of the inspiration of stars, the dignity of the moon, and the lullabies of crickets and frogs.

Let us restore the night and reclaim it as a sanctuary of peace, where silence shall be music to our hearts and darkness shall throw light upon our souls. Good night. Sweet dreams. Amen.[2]

30

*T*he Storms
Will Disappear

Be merciful to me, O LORD, for I am in distress; my eyes grow weak with sorrow, my soul and my body with grief. My life is consumed by anguish and my years are groaning; my strength fails because of my affliction, and my bones grow weak (Psalm 31:9-10).

Graphic isn't it? It's a description of mourning. It's neither a comfortable place nor one we'd purposely choose. It's painful, confusing, and frightening. Part of the fear comes from not knowing if what we're feeling or experiencing is normal or if we're going crazy.

You will mourn in your own unique way, and it could change from day to day. You may be a person who prefers stability and a set routine, or you may prefer variation. What you experience now may be totally different tomorrow.

Grieving takes many forms and expressions. Your cultural background will affect its expression. For some, wailing is their style while for others there will be no public expression. Sometimes you're aware of your emotions. Other times they affect you but there's no awareness. This, too, is normal.

A singer and writer suffered the death of his fiancé. See what his emotional journey was like.

> I moved to a vacant lot, at least emotionally. All the dreams and plans and longings were leveled to the horizon and beyond. The season in my heart changed to winter and refused to allow spring to come for over two years. Out of the sheer pain and shock, the whys and what ifs, the sleepless nights, the wrestling match with God, the test of faith, two questions emerged. The first, simply one of survival: Is there a way through? The second, which came much later: Is there a way back? To live? To feel? To joy? Or would I become one among the masses, quietly desperate, subtly (or openly) cynical, trudging toward the ultimate and only relief, death and heaven beyond?[1]

Sometime later he was able to pen these words that can give us hope:

> Little by little the storms became fewer and farther apart. The stars broke through. And many months later, after more than a year had passed, something happened. The tears began to change. And I hope and pray that this happens in you, too.
>
> At some point—and it can be a long while in coming, in one of those moments when that certain song comes on the radio or when you round that familiar bend in the road where you walked, talked, ate, laughed, or played with the one who is now safe in the arms of heaven—as the agony of separation wells up inside you like a physical hurt—your tears will change. A certain alchemy like water into wine will occur. The tears will turn from reflections of misery to jewels of tribute. They will no longer be mostly streams of self-pity, but will shine with honor to the one you miss. All

the self-pity may never be gone, just as the finest diamond has flaws that make it unique. But you will know when it happens. You will have what C.S. Lewis called "clean and honest" agony, "good and tonic" moments. The sky will begin to clear. The color will creep back into the landscape.

And even before you are fully aware of it, a mysterious thing will happen. You will do what you fear most—let go a little more. A step back into the land of the living will logically seem like a step farther from the one you mourn. But in letting go—and this is the mysterious part—you will be moved nearer to, not farther from, the fields of heaven and the ones you know there. You will sense how thin the veil is between this world and the next—a curtain held up by only a string of heartbeats. And instead of wishing your heart stopped, the steadiness of your beating heart will call you back to this life like a universal Morse code.[2]

31

God, Where Are You?

God, where are you?"

"I'm here."

That is his answer. Sometimes when grief hits we wonder where God is, or we feel alienated. We feel the weight of the loss rather than the hope of relief. Right now you may feel distanced from God or you may feel closer. In grief, we need something for our stability. Again and again Scripture gives us the comfort we long for as it talks about God's compassionate heart.

> Though he brings grief, he will show compassion, so great is his unfailing love. For he does not willingly bring affliction or grief to the children of men (Lamentations 3:32-33).

> Blessed are those who mourn, for they will be comforted (Matthew 5:4).

> But you, O God, do see trouble and grief; you consider it to take it in hand. The victim commits himself to you; you are the helper of the fatherless (Psalm 10:14).

> Your sun will never set again, and your moon will wane no more; the LORD will be your everlasting light, and your days of sorrow will end (Isaiah 60:20).

> Because I have said these things, you are filled with

grief....I tell you the truth, you will weep and mourn while the world rejoices. You will grieve, but *your grief will turn to joy* (John 16:6,20).

For we do not have a high priest who is *unable to sympathize* with our weaknesses, but we have one who has been tempted in every way, just as we are—yet was without sin (Hebrews 4:15).

Your world is probably not the world you want it to be at this time of your life. God is in the process of remaking your world into something that will be different and in many ways better. He will help you by giving you strength, grace, and a surrounding sense of his love.

God's love will show itself around you in small ways. And little by little that great love will grow like the dawn, warm you, and draw you forward toward the horizon. God, the Father of us all, and no stranger to a wounded heart, loves you. And someday this canyon that he is bringing you through will be a monument to the power of that love.

Take heart, wounded friend. Take time to grieve, but grieve and hope. Cry a river. An ocean if you like. "Take a hand kindly offered. Help one faint robin. Keep tying your shoes. Read the psalms or have someone read them to you. Find some good walking companions and some good traveling songs. Here is one of mine. Sometimes I hear it sung from earth to heaven. Sometimes I think it's what those already there are singing to us.

I don't want to let you go
I don't want to say goodbye,
But the road he's led us here to this divide
Nothing I can say or do

Can make it any other way
But the promise of forever knows no time or space
And out there in the somewhere will I pray
And speak your name....Every day to heaven
Now Go, shine like a star
Knowing our hearts can never really be apart
Fly as high as you can
And it won't be long
'Til I see you again
What is meant to be is such a mystery
And mysteries are not meant to understand
The hardest part of love has got to be
Leaving it in bigger hands[1]

$\mathcal{A}$ Time for Tears

Our son died in 1990. His life and death taught my wife and me about loss and grief. Matthew was profoundly mentally retarded and died at the age of 22. Tears were plentiful for years.

I found two written responses to my tears that I had put in a folder. This first one I wrote nine months after Matthew's death:

> January 5, 1991
>
> Where have the tears gone? There was a time when I thought they would never end, but now I miss them as though they were a friend. There's only a mist where once a stream, the memories are fading all too fast, like it was last night's dream. It seems too soon to be this way, but I realize they may return yet another day. Who would have thought the sobs and clouded eyes would be missed, but they are. And yet, even as this is written, the words are difficult to see for some strange reason.
>
> The poems and letters from friends help to bring back the loss again. Words of comfort expressed at the time of deepest pain help to keep Matthew's memory alive. For that's all we have of him now—memories. Someone else has the joy of his presence, his laugh, his smile, and his hugs.
>
> Where have the tears gone? They haven't. They were hiding and waiting once again for the time to be called out and help express the loss. They're here again, not as an intruder,

but as a welcomed friend. Please don't stay away so long the next time. I need you. We need you….

Then in the fifteenth month, I wrote,

It's been some time since the feelings came to the surface. You begin to wonder if they ever will again. But then they do. And each time is different. It began with finding some old pictures of Matthew when he was quite young and in most of them he was smiling. Two days later, we were watching Dr. Ogilvie on a Sunday morning TV program, and he read the passage in which the centurion came to Jesus about his son who was dying. Jesus told him to go home, his son would live. Both my wife and I had the same response: "I wish Jesus would have made that statement to us about Matthew." The tears came that morning. They will always be there and come when we least expect them. But they are there as part of our connection with something that we valued but lost, at least for the present time. They are also a reminder that our life is a series of transitions and changes, some of which we like and others we resist.

You can recover. It will take an understanding of the grief process, a change of attitude from thinking *It will never end* to *I will adjust and survive,* and a willingness to make the painful journey through the wilderness of grief.

Ann Kaiser Stearns says, "All of us feel powerless at times because we are human beings. Triumphant survivors, however, trade in the position of helplessness for a decision to take charge and search for options."[1]

Be patient with your recovery, but believe you will recover. David Wiersbe offers good advice about believing:

In grief God seems to have abandoned us. He hasn't. In grief we feel as if nothing matters. It does. Sometimes we think life is not worth living: It is! In times of sorrow, people of faith have to "believe against the grain." In our weakness, God reveals his strength, and we do more than we thought possible.

Faith means clinging to God in spite of circumstances. It means following him when we cannot see, being faithful to him when we don't feel like it.

Mourners need a creed—it is "I believe!" We need to affirm this creed daily:

- I believe God's promises are true.

- I believe heaven is real.

- I believe I will see my child again.

- I believe God will see me through.

- I believe nothing can separate me from God's love.

- I believe God has work for me to do.

"Believing against the grain," means having a survivalist attitude. Bereaved parents are survivors; they have endured. Not only do they survive, but also out of grief they create something good.[2]

33

A Psalm of Lament

*L*ament. It's not a common word. Most of us don't use it in everyday speech. And yet when we're in grief, we do it. Over a dozen different Hebrew words are translated as "lament." It means to mourn or express deep sorrow, grief, or contrition. In Hebrew life, public lamentation was common. In Amos we read, "There will be wailing in all the streets and cries of anguish in every public square. The farmers will be summoned to weep and the mourners to wail" (Amos 5:16).

The Jewish or Mideastern pattern of mourning is very healthy because people give expression to their feelings. They don't edit what they say. We don't need to either. The following psalm of lament is not from Scripture, but from the heart of one who experienced a loss. Read it aloud and then compare it to your own situation. It's another way to experience God's comfort.

> Night after night
> I collect my tears
> and send them to you, O God.
> Night after night
> I come before you,
> tear-stained.
> Have mercy on me.
> Hear my weeping

and turn your heart to me.
I weep for what was
and will never be again.
I weep for a future
that is no longer possible.
I weep because I love.
Like a willow
on the bank of a river,
I'm bent
from the weight of my tears.
They flood my world,
and there is no stopping
their force.
Save me, O God, from drowning!
O God,
have you covered your ears
to my weeping?
Have you covered your eyes
so you won't see me
going under?
Have you forgotten me
night after night?
Didn't you hear your son
weeping over Jerusalem?
Didn't you count his tears
when Lazarus died?
Didn't you see
how deeply moved he was
when Mary wept?
O God, acknowledge me,
for night after night
I collect my tears
and send them to you.

I trust in you, O God,
for your hand

can divide the waters,
or gently wipe the tears
of the grieving ones.
I trust you, O God,
day after day.[1]

*Y*ou Are Special

Do you feel like a special person at this time or like someone who is being picked on? When you're in a crisis state or dealing with a loss, it's more like feeling picked on and not in a positive way. Keep in mind that no matter what is happening in your life right now, you are special—more special than you realize. And not only that, God wants the best for you even though it may not seem that way at this time.

Let's look at God's Word:

> Surely goodness and love will follow me all the days of my life, and I will dwell in the house of the LORD forever (Psalm 23:6).

> I will make an everlasting covenant with them: I will never stop doing good to them....I will rejoice in doing them good and will assuredly plant them in this land with all my heart and soul (Jeremiah 32:40-41).

Our understanding of who God is and how he wants to bless our lives is enriched when we realize that he is committed to performing good in our lives.

A few years ago, the choir at our church sang an anthem based on Zephaniah 3:17. I had never heard the song before. The words were printed in our church bulletin, and I have read them many times because they encourage me, inspire me, and remind me of what I mean to God:

> And the Father will dance over you in joy!
> He will take delight in whom He loves.
> Is that a choir I hear singing the praises of God?
> No, the Lord God Himself is exulting over you in song!
> And He will joy over you in song!
> My soul will make its boast in God,
> For He has answered all my cries.
> His faithfulness to me is as sure as the dawn of
>   a new day.
> Awake my soul and sing!
> Let my spirit rejoice in God!
> Sing, O daughter of Zion, with all of your heart!
> Cast away the fear for you have been restored!
> Put on the garment of praise as on a festival day.
> Join with the Father in glorious, jubilant song.
> God rejoices over you in song.[1]

In his fascinating book *The Pleasures of God*, John Piper beautifully expresses how God desires to do good to all who hope in him. Dr. Piper talks about God singing and asks, "What would it be like if God sang?":

> What do you hear when you imagine the voice of God singing?
>
> I hear the booming of Niagara Falls mingled with the trickle of a mossy mountain stream. I hear the blast of Mt. St. Helens mingled with a kitten's purr. I hear the power of an East Coast hurricane and the barely audible puff of a night snow in the woods. And I hear the unimaginable roar of the sun, 865,000 miles thick; 1,300,000 times bigger than the earth; and nothing but fire, 1,000,000 degrees centigrade on the

cooler surface of the corona. But I hear this unimaginable roar mingled with the tender, warm crackling of logs in the living room on a cozy winter's night.

I stand dumbfounded, staggered, speechless that he is singing over me—one who has dishonored him so many times and in so many ways. It is almost too good to be true. He is rejoicing over my good with all his heart and all his soul. He virtually breaks forth into song when he hits upon a new way to do me good.[2]

Did you catch the significance of how God feels about *you* and what He wants for you? Do you get a sense of the blessing for which you have been created and chosen?

Does that say something to you about your value and worth? Does that fling open the doors of possibility for you to make choices in your life that will lead to hope and eventually to change and blessing? It can.

Remind yourself of this again and again. It will give you a better day.

The Slowness of Grief

Grief is filled with the unexpected—we respond in new ways, think new thoughts, feel new feelings, and are just not ourselves. We tend to fight it every inch of the way because it's just not "who we were." And so we feel uncomfortable. But the truth is, we need whatever we're experiencing. Yes, we actually need what is occurring because it helps us heal.

We need the tears of grief. Our tears give voice to what our words fail to express. Without the drainage of tears, there are likely to be volcano-sized eruptions later on when the lid comes off. Tears are not synonymous with a lack of faith nor are they a sign of despair. Tears never need an explanation or an apology.

We also need the slowness of grief. When grief hits, it's as though someone put a slowdown switch on every clock we see. No matter what you try, it won't speed up the process. A friend, Joyce Landorf Heatherly, described it so well:

> Time feels like it has come to a complete stop after we lose a loved one. The most unbearable stretch of the day seems to be in those dark hours just before daybreak. It's so cold, so dark, and so forbidding that time of the day, our anxiety gets thick enough to cut with a knife.

However, do not be impatient with the slowness of grief's music. Its *largo* tempo (which plods along at a maddening slow pace) may be very essential for a healthy recovery. We long for the upbeat tempo of what we recognize as "normal" for our life's melody, but it may take a very long time to finally play out grief's song.

If we rush this time of adjusting along too fast, we rob grief of the work of the gradual healing it must carry out. We must not be in such a hurry to get ourselves or our bereaved friends "back to normal." It is essential to remember "normal" has been forever altered into abnormal. We do the bereaved an injustice when we do not allow them to grieve. And since we need to grieve, if we are not allowed to, we create yet another problem: *guilt*. The bereaved do not want to walk away from a gravesite and bring down a mental curtain, shutting off forever the person who has died. That is cruel and somehow seems to be a very unloyal thing to do. This causes the guilty feeling in the bereaved of not being true or faithful to the deceased. They must be encouraged to talk, express their feelings—whether they be sad, angry, or lonely—and take all the time they need. The natural slowness of grief cooperates here and can be a useful tool toward adjustments in living.[1]

We also need to accept the apathy of grief. You don't have the energy, the drive, or the desire to do much at this time. It's a struggle just to get through the day, and formerly simple tasks seem overwhelming. Your decision-making is a labor now. C.S. Lewis described this apathy as the "laziness of grief." Give yourself permission not to be yourself and don't expect much. Ask others to help. Let others minister to you at this time.

We also need to see grief as a creative gift. Out of grief our values change and often new dreams unfold. It may be difficult to believe that now, but a new day does arrive. If you can accept these factors, then comfort can accompany your pain and uneasiness. There are always different tomorrows.

36

Overcoming Fear

Fear. With losses and grief, fears begin to creep into our lives. The "what ifs" find a foothold. What if I stay like this forever? What if I don't get better? What if another loss comes into my life? What if no one helps me? Those who recover are those who confront their fears, identify them, put them in perspective, and allow them to diminish slowly while they focus on positive improvement. Many survivors have found it helpful to list each of their fears and place a check by it each time it occurs. It also helps to identify what you used to fear and how you overcame it.

There's nothing that helps one to overcome fear as much as concentrating upon God's Word and committing it to memory. God can use passages such as Isaiah 41:10; 43:1; Philippians 4:6-9; and Psalm 37:1-10 to bring you the peace you are looking for. Never avoid or give in to your fears because each time you do so, fear grows. Face fear, admit you're fearful, and then evict it.

Years ago I was privileged to meet a pastor's wife, the author of an inspiring article about a letter she wrote to her children. The letter expressed how she was struggling with a recurrence of cancer. In one part of the letter she talked about fear:

> Fear has knocked at my door. Sometimes in the past five days I have let fear in for a while. It has not been good. I have thought of silly things like: I can't wear

that new spring suit we just bought on sale or that lovely wool skirt we've waited six months for. Other times I think how much I want to see Kathy graduate, go off to Bible school, fall in love with the finest Christian man this world has ever seen, and then watch her walk down the aisle on her dad's arm. Then I think I want to see Kim married and settled. Finally, for sure, I would like grandchildren.

But, dear children of mine, these are human thoughts, and to dwell on them is not healthy. I know one of the strongest desires God has given us is the desire to live, but I want to say to God that I trust Him in this too. My vision is so limited. These human desires are the purest on earth, but if I had even a tiny glimpse of heaven I wouldn't want to stay here. Because I am human, I do. So I have decided to put a "No Trespassing" sign at the entrance of the path of human desires and not let my thoughts wander down it.

When fear knocks, it is my determined choice to let faith answer the door, faith that is settled on the sure promise of the Word of God.[1]

How can you accomplish this kind of settled decision? Sometimes it means asking others for help. Your fear could have a useful component to it. It could prompt you to make some necessary changes that could have a positive impact on your life.

37

*W*orship Brings Comfort

~

Have you ever thought how worshiping God can give you comfort? That's where Job found his greatest consolation.

In one day, Job lost everything—his servants, his livestock, his wealth, and his children. "At this, Job got up and tore his robe and shaved his head. Then he fell to the ground in worship and said: 'Naked I came from my mother's womb, and naked I will depart. The LORD gave and the LORD has taken away; may the name of the LORD be praised.' In all this Job did not sin by charging God with wrongdoing" (Job 1:20-22).[1]

We don't worship God because of our losses, but in spite of them. We don't praise Him for the tragedies, but in them. Like Job, we hear God speak to us out of the storm (Job 38:1). Like the disciples at sea in a small boat caught in a severe storm, we see Jesus coming to us in the fourth watch of the night. We hear Him say, "Take courage! It is I. Don't be afraid" (Matthew 14:27).

If you've lived for any length of time, you've probably had opportunity to see the different ways people respond to adversity. The same tragedy can make one person better and another person bitter. What makes the difference? Resources. Inner resources developed across a lifetime though spiritual disciplines. *If you haven't worshiped regularly in the sunshine of your life, you probably won't be able to worship in the darkness.* If you haven't been intimate with God in life's ordinariness, it's not likely that you will know how or where to find Him should life hand you some real hardships. *But by the same token, if you have worshiped often and regularly, then you will undoubtedly worship well in the hour of your greatest need.*[2]

The experience of worship provides the deep resources we need to draw upon when everything around us falls apart. In worship, the emphasis and focus is not upon you but upon God. Do you realize that your theology will affect how you respond to loss? Your response to life's losses will be directly determined by your understanding of God and how you have worshiped.

Often we don't feel like worshiping God when we're grieving. But that's where to begin. "God, I don't feel like doing this, but in spite of what happened, I'll do what Job did. I will praise you and honor you. I will begin by worshiping."

We are people who usually put faith in formulas. We feel comfortable with predictability, regularity, and assurance. We want God to be this way also, and so we try to create him in the image of what we want him to be and what we want him to do.

However, you and I cannot predict what God will do. Paul reminds us of that in Romans 11:33: "O the depth of the riches both of the wisdom and knowledge of God! how unsearchable are his judgments, and his ways past finding out!" (KJV).

God is not uncaring or busy elsewhere. He is neither insensitive nor punitive. He is supreme, sovereign, loving, and sensitive.

I don't fully comprehend God. I, too, have unanswered questions about some of the events of my life.

38

$\mathcal{I}$ Wish...

Unfinished business—it's not uncommon for a person to think, "I wish we could have talked about that and settled that issue," or "I wish I would have…" Many feel incomplete because of some unfinished business and that could be causing some regrets. After a while we begin to carry these regrets around like unwanted burdens.

Those in grief often carry baggage that weighs them down. If you have regrets, identify them. Write them down in order to clarify what they are and face them. A prayer to offer is: "Almighty God, to you all hearts are open, all desires known, and from you no secrets are hid. I bring to you this troubling memory.[1] Another way to identify what could be bothering you is to complete the following sentences as many times as necessary:

"I wasn't the best…"
"I wish I would have…"

Here is another prayer that has been offered for centuries and has been comforting to many.

All that we ought to have thought,
   and have not thought.
All that we ought to have said,
   and have not said.

All that we ought to have done,
   and have not done.
All that we ought not to have thought,
   and yet have thought.
All that we ought not to have spoken,
   and yet have spoken.
All that we ought not to have done,
   and yet have done.
For thoughts, words and works, pray we,
   O God, for Forgiveness.[2]

39

The Goodness of Grief

Grief is a love word. It may not seem that way but it is. One thought to keep in mind that can bring you comfort is God grieves with us. Think about this for a moment. The psalmist said, "How often they provoked Him in the wilderness, and grieved Him in the desert!" (Psalm 78:40 NKJV).

It's true. God grieves when his people rebel or disobey. Paul said, "Do not grieve the Holy Spirit of God, by whom you were sealed for the day of redemption. Let all bitterness, wrath, anger, clamor, and evil speaking be put away from you, with all malice" (Ephesians 4:30-31). God the Father, the Son, and the Holy Spirit grieve when we refuse to respond to God's guidelines.

Grief is natural. It is desirable. We were created with the ability to grieve. Grief can help us realize our own capacity to give and to receive love. Sometimes in all the admonitions and guidelines he gives, we forget that Paul was a man who also grieved. He said, "Out of much affliction and anguish of heart I wrote to you, with many tears, not that you should be grieved, but that you might know the love which I have so abundantly for you" (2 Corinthians 2:4). Another version says, "...I did not write to make you sad, but to let you know how much I love you" (NCV).

Grief is a way of expressing love, and the intensity of grief is directly related to the intensity of love. The more you love a person, the more intense your grief.

Grief puts you in a position to depend upon God, to trust him for healing and restoration. It's easy to end up thinking, "No one else can understand what I'm feeling and the extent of my loss." On one hand, you're right. It's difficult for another person to enter into your grief with you. But God knows and he is waiting for you to go to him for comfort and for healing. Were you aware the psalmist says that God collects your tears in a bottle (Psalm 56:8 NASB)? He doesn't ignore your tears. He sees them and remembers them. Jeremiah, the prophet said,

> For men are not cast off by the Lord forever:
> Though he brings grief, he will show compassion
> so great is his unfailing love.
> For he does not willingly bring affliction
> or grief to the children of men
> (Lamentations 3:31-33).

God is a God of compassion. Is your hurt or grief so deep you wonder if you're ever going to be able to climb out of the pit? The answer is yes you will.

In the midst of grief, God has something good for you. He is in your grief with you. When will you discover what it is? No one can tell you. What you can remember is, God knows and in his timing he will let you know.[1]

40

Saying Goodbye

How many times in your life have you said "Goodbye"? You probably can't remember. None of us can. This expression is as much a part of life as day passing into night and then back into day again. Children and parents say it to one another each day when they go their separate ways.

The word *goodbye*, originally "God-be-with-ye" or "Go-with-God," was a recognition that God was a part of the going. For those embarking upon a journey that was unknown or even dreaded, it reminded them God was there and gave strength. There was the belief that God would be there to protect and comfort.

When some leave us, even though we know we will see them again, there is pain. Sending a child off to college is filled with both joy and sadness. We know it's good, it's necessary, it's a transition, but our goodbyes at that time are intense.

> Goodbyes are a part of every single day. Sometimes we choose them, and sometimes they choose us. Usually they are small, insignificant losses that do not pain us very much, but at times they are deep, powerful, wounding experiences that trail around our heart and keep pain inside of us for years.
>
> What is a goodbye? It is an empty place in us. It is any situation in which there is some kind of loss.[1]

There are goodbyes we don't want to say. Some are so final we avoid the words. Sometimes we're not ready to say the words until weeks or months after a loved one has died. We hold out for a better ending to the story than the one that was just written. When you are forced to say goodbye, you resist it, hoping what happened isn't true. It's an attempt to block out the pain, but doing this can also block out memories of the loved one. Yes, saying goodbye is painful, but it allows you to move through and past your pain and into healing. A woman said, "I did not know how hard it would be to say goodbye. Yet it was harder still when I refused to say it."[2]

Take comfort in the fact that not wanting to say goodbye is normal. Take comfort in the fact that saying goodbye does not mean you don't love the person. And take comfort in the fact your goodbyes are temporary, for one day you will say hello again in a new place.

41

The Night Shift

Nighttime. For most it's a time of rest when the body and mind slow down. As the darkness intensifies, noises diminish and quiet takes over. At least for most people. Then there are those who work the night shift. When others are asleep, these individuals are wide awake and hard at work. It could be a nurse on an ER ward or a baker preparing tomorrow's breads. It could be a road crew trying to repair damage while traffic isn't so intense. It's the police officers cruising the streets of a darkened city and the firemen and paramedics running for their trucks as a call comes in.

Others aren't on-call or working, but they're awake just the same. Sleep is elusive when you're hurting and grief is your constant companion. You try to sleep, but it won't come. Or you get to sleep, finally hoping for a reprieve from the pain, but it follows you and troubles your dreams. So you awake as tired as you were before you slept.

You have your own night shift you didn't apply for. There's someone else who works the night shift, too. His name is God. Had you ever thought about God working the late shift? While you're sleeping or wrestling with sleep, God is busy. He's ever-present and caring about you at all times. The psalmist's words can bring you comfort: "He who watches over you will not slumber; indeed, he who watches over Israel will neither slumber nor sleep" (Psalm 121:3-4).

There are both promises and guidelines within God's words that speak to our sleep and rest.

> When you lie down, you won't be afraid; when you lie down, your sleep will be sweet (Proverbs 3:24).

> I lie down and sleep. I wake again, because the LORD sustains me....I will lie down and sleep in peace, for you alone, O LORD, make me dwell in safety (Psalm 3:5; 4:8).

Author Ron Mehl talks about God's activities at night while we're sleeping or attempting to sleep. " 'The one who never sleeps' is the God who moves outside our vision and occupies Himself with tasks beyond our comprehension. His eyes peer into what we can't see and His hands work skillfully where we can only grope. This is the God who reaches and thinks and plans and shapes and watches and controls and feels and acts while we're unconscious under a sheet and a comforter."[1]

When you wake up, go to these thoughts: God has been at work. He has been thinking about you. This sustained David again and again. "How precious it is, Lord, to realize that you are thinking about me constantly. I can't even count how many times a day your thoughts turn toward me. And when I waken in the morning, you are still thinking of me" (Psalm 139:17-18 TLB).

> Remember, when you wonder where God is, He is here, always.
> God is aware of your circumstances, and moves among them.
> God is aware of your pain, and monitors every second of it.

God is aware of your emptiness, and seeks to fill it in
a manner beyond your dreams.

God is aware of your wounds and scars and knows
how to draw forth a healing deeper than you can
imagine.

Yes, God works the night shift.

Even when nothing seems to be moving in your darkness,

Even when your situation seems out of control,

Even when you feel alone and afraid.[2]

If you can't sleep, talk to God. It helps.

42

Express Your Questions

~

As you look at others going about the routine of their daily lives, do you ever wonder why life stopped for you? Everyone else seems to be moving on and your entire life has been disrupted. Does it cross your mind? Probably. Everyone has questions. Often, for one reason or another, they're not voiced. They need to be. Not that they'll be answered, but they need to be expressed, especially to God. The following prayer may help you put into words what may be churning around on the inside. Read this prayer aloud for several days. It can make a difference.

> O God,
> Sometimes I can't help wondering
> why this should have happened to me.
> You get a lot of time to think
> when you are struggling with grief.
> And sometimes I can't help wondering
> > why there is so much suffering and pain in the world.
> I know that there just isn't any answer to these questions,
> > at least not now.
> So help me to accept
> > what I can't understand.

And help me to be sure
    that this is not the only world,
and that there is some place
    where broken hearts are mended,
    where the lost things are found,
    where all the problems are solved,
    where we know, even as we are known.
So in this world help me to leave it all to you,
in the certainty that I will never be tired
    beyond what you will make me able to bear. Amen.[1]

Lord, give me the psalmist's certainty:

Even though I walk through the valley of the shadow of death, I will fear no evil; for Thou art with me; Thy rod and Thy staff, they comfort me (Psalm 23:4 NASB).

In heavenly love abiding,
No change my heart shall fear;
And safe in such confiding,
For nothing changes here;
The storm may roar without me,
My heart may low be laid;
But God is round about me,
And can I be dismayed?

—Anna L. Waring
"In Heavenly Love Abiding"

43

Relearn Your World

What is the story of your life? Have you ever thought about it, let alone shared it with others? What if we all had to write our life story? What would it contain? What would the common thread be that would connect all of us? I think it would be the experience of loss. And when you experience loss and move into grief, you experience a disruption and incompleteness. Loss disrupts your life story. Life isn't as it was nor will it be. This is a time when you are struggling to discover a new sense and direction to the continuing story of your life.

Grief is a time of relearning your world. You will relearn your relationship with other family members and friends who also have been impacted by this loss. Some may move closer to you, while others shy away as they struggle, not knowing what to do or say. Those at work, church, and in the businesses you frequent have to learn new ways of responding to you as well. They wonder if they should mention the one you lost by name and hope you are back to "normal" in three to four months. Some of your former "comfortable" relationships are challenged now.

You also need to relearn who you are since the loss you experienced. If your loss was a significant person, then how you used to refer to yourself may not be the same.

You may be relearning your life as it relates to time and space. Some spend more of their time in the past with memories and pictures than the present and especially the future. It could be guilt from the past that blocks thoughts of the future. Significant dates and holidays will impact you in a way you've never experienced before. Avoidance and sorrow could be your struggles at this time. Certain places in your home and community that used to be wholesome and safe now are too painful to experience so you avoid them.

And you will be relearning your relationship with God. This can range from deep questions and feelings of abandonment to a renewed faith and a search for meaning in whatever happened. Yes, grief can shake you spiritually, but you can experience your loss and all these adjustments as a "tragic opportunity." Your loss will eventually allow you to become a person who you have never been before and touch the lives of others in a way that could never have occurred previously. Don't worry if you can't see this possibility at this time, that's all right.

Take comfort—if you are experiencing what has been described, you are normal. Loss is confusing and disruptive, and our lives are turned upside down. But you will survive. You will grow. You will be used to touch others.

> Blessed be the God and Father of our Lord Jesus Christ, the Father of sympathy (pity and mercy) and the God [Who is the Source] of every comfort (consolation and encouragement), Who comforts (consoles and encourages) us in every trouble (calamity and affliction), so that we may also be able to comfort (console and encourage) those who are in any kind of trouble *or* distress, with the comfort (consolation and encouragement) with which we ourselves are comforted (consoled and encouraged) by God. For just as Christ's [own] sufferings fall to our lot [as

they overflow upon His disciples, and we share and experience them] abundantly, so through Christ comfort (consolation and encouragement) is also [shared and experienced] abundantly by us (2 Corinthians 1:3-5 AMP).

44

Seek Ye First...

> But seek first his kingdom and his righteousness, and all these things will be given to you as well (Matthew 6:33).

This may seem like a strange verse to think about when the dominating concern in a grieving person's mind is relief. But grief can be so consuming. Isn't it easy to forget not only what we've been taught but who even taught us? Our priorities may shift when we're upset. Perhaps in the midst of whatever is going on, it helps to be called back to some basics.

Jesus said two things in Matthew 6:33—that the Christian life represents seeking his kingdom and seeking his righteousness. And yes, even in the midst of our upset, Jesus is talking about priorities. Sometimes in our grief, we become frantic in our quest to recover and overcome the pain. In fact, it's easy to become dominated by worry.

In Matthew 6:25-28, Jesus talks about the simple things of life, like birds, flowers, life, food, and the body. In verse 34, he simply says, "Don't worry about tomorrow." In other words, don't forget your priorities. Focus on him and his kingdom rather than worrying. In the midst of your upset ask, "How can I still seek Jesus' kingdom and his righteousness?" Perhaps it's simply having faith in the basics. Jesus said, "Love the Lord your God with all your heart and with all your soul and with all your mind...[And] love your neighbor as yourself" (Matthew 22:37,39). What would happen if you reminded yourself of this several times a day?

Some friends of mine suggested the following:

> Jesus is telling us that, in a certain sense, living the Christian life is very simple. Just rest in God's grace. Be like the birds of the air or the flowers of the field. Fly free. Bloom on the hillside of your life. Have faith that no matter what happens in your life, you are a child of the king. And as you seek the king's "kingdom" and his lifestyle, you will discover that all the rest of your needs will be taken care of. He will work through you and with you to use your gifts and abilities as well as your circumstances to provide for your every need. "Trust me," says Christ, "I *really* will take care of you."

> Dear Lord, I must admit that trusting you alone is a pretty big challenge. Deep in my heart I believe fully that you will care for me regardless of my situation. But I also know that my attention can be easily diverted from that trust. Sometimes I feel very much like the men Jesus met who confessed, "I do believe; help me overcome my unbelief!" (Mark 9:24). Strengthen my ability to trust you, because only you know what lies in my future, and only you can ultimately help me through my earthly life into the eternal home you have promised. Amen.[1]

45

Suffering and God's Promises

Storms are never pleasant—their nature is to unsettle, destroy, confuse, and wreak havoc. Part of our ability to endure these inevitable storms is in our outlook. From the apostle Paul, we learn much about suffering; we discover from him a new view.

Suffering is not impossible to endure. The severity of the dangers Paul encountered is unbelievable (see 2 Corinthians 11:24-28); yet, even in expressing the pressures he felt, he consistently maintained that they were not unbearable:

> We are hard pressed on every side, but not crushed; perplexed, but not in despair; persecuted, but not abandoned; struck down, but not destroyed (2 Corinthians 4:8-9).

By claiming that storms are not impossible to endure, I in no way am minimizing the severity of the storm or the destruction that it brings. We just need to keep in mind we have promises from God that he will not give us more than we can bear and that he will always provide a way out so that we can stand up under it.

Suffering is momentary. Paul was able to view suffering as momentary because he saw it as part of a larger picture. He knew the important part of the picture was in the realm of the unseen, and this is where he tells us to fix our eyes.

Therefore we do not lose heart. Though outwardly we are wasting away, yet inwardly we are being renewed day by day. For our light and momentary troubles are achieving for us an eternal glory that far outweighs them all. So we fix our eyes not on what is seen, but on what is unseen. For what is seen is temporary, but what is unseen is eternal (2 Corinthians 4:16-18).

Suffering brings our future reward into clear view. Abraham was able to endure difficulty because he was "looking forward to the city with foundations, whose architect and builder is God" (Hebrews 11:10). Moses was able to endure mistreatment because he looked ahead to his reward with eyes of faith.

By faith Moses...regarded disgrace for the sake of Christ as of greater value than the treasures of Egypt, because he was looking ahead to his reward (Hebrews 11:24-26).

Suffering must be viewed through eyes of trust. Trusting God when we can't see his hand or hear his voice requires all the faith we can muster. You may identify with the pain and frustration in the following words from David. Notice his concluding thoughts.

How long, O LORD? Will you forget me forever?
    How long will you hide your face from me?
How long must I wrestle with my thoughts
    and every day have sorrow in my heart?
    How long will my enemy triumph over me?
Look on me and answer, O LORD my God.
    Give light to my eyes, or I will sleep in death;
my enemy will say, "I have overcome him,"
    and my foes will rejoice when I fall.
But I trust in your unfailing love;
    my heart rejoices in your salvation.

> I will sing to the LORD,
>> for he has been good to me (Psalm 13:1-6).

In all that David went through, he continued to trust in God and to proclaim his goodness. He looked beyond the present and trusted God to keep his promises.[1]

46

*U*nique in Your Grief

~

I'm not grieving like others I know, what is wrong with me?"
Probably nothing. Most wonder about this because grief can be so
new. You are a unique person, and this uniqueness comes into
play. The type or quality of the relationship you had with
whomever you lost will also affect how you grieve. How close or
involved you were with the person will affect you. The closer a
person was, the more intense the grief and the more you may
need to restructure your life. You may be observing other people
whose relationships with the one who is gone weren't as close and
wonder why their grief is different than yours. Others' grief may
be not as intense or last as long. It's easy to begin questioning your
own responses. Don't compare yourself with others.

Other factors will impact your response. If this is the first
major loss of your life, everything is so new. This in itself will create more questions and uncertainty. If you've experienced prior
major losses, how you dealt with them plays a part. If you sur-
vived well and learned from your losses in a positive way, you have
something to fall back on. If not, this present situation may create
a sense of dread and anxiety. Each loss has the potential to make
you a stronger person—or it could have just the opposite effect. If
your pattern in life has been to confront challenges and problems,

you'll probably do that with this loss. If your style is to avoid, this will probably emerge as your response.

Your personality will also come into play. If you tend to be more of a thinker and respond to life by analyzing, looking at the facts, and making decisions with your head, why should you be any different when you're grieving? Or you could respond to life based upon your feelings and make decisions according to your heart rather than your head. This would cause a different response to grief.

You could also be one who goes into great detail when you talk and give novel-length responses to a simple "How are you?" Or it could be just the opposite. You may be sparse with your words and deliberate in what you say. We are all different, and these differences are evident in our grief.

Give yourself permission to be unique in your grief and your expression of what you are experiencing. God does not judge the way and manner in which we grieve, so why should we?

47

*T*he Choices in Loss

There's another side to loss. It takes time to discover it. It could be weeks, months, or even years, but it does happen. What is said here may be encouraging or unbelievable or annoying or infuriating. It depends on where you are in your grief. Listen to the words of a man who lost his mother, his wife, and a daughter in an auto accident. He has been there.

> It is therefore not true that we become less through loss—unless we allow the loss to make us less, grinding our soul down until there is nothing left but an external self entirely under the control of circumstances. Loss can also make us more. In the darkness, we can still find the light. In death, we can also find life. It depends on the choices we make. Though these choices are difficult and rarely made in haste or with ease, we can nevertheless make them. Only when we choose to pay attention to our souls will we learn how much more there is to life than the external world around us, however wonderful or horrible that world is. We will discover the world within. Yet such attention to the soul does not have to engender self-absorption. If anything, it eventually turns us toward the

world again and makes us more compassionate and just than we might have otherwise been.

Loss provides an opportunity to take inventory of our lives, to reconsider priorities, and to determine new directions. "Few people," someone once told me, "wish at seventy that they had worked more hours at the office when they were forty. If anything, they wish that they had given more time back then to family, friends, and worthy causes. They wish they had dared to say 'no' to pressure, competition and image and 'no' to their own selfishness." As Jesus said, "What good is it for a man to gain the whole world, and yet forfeit his soul?" Loss invites us to ask basic questions about ourselves. "What do I believe?" "Is there life after death?" "Is there a God?" "What kind of person am I?" "Do I really care about other people?" "How have I used my resources—my time, money, and talent?" "Where am I headed with my life?"

Deep sorrow is good for the soul for another reason, too. It can make us more alive to the present moment. This notion may appear to contradict what I mentioned earlier. But perhaps the present is other than the nothingness it has sometimes seemed to be. It may be that the present contains the secret of the renewal of life we long for, as if, in looking under the surface of this vast sea of nothingness, we may find another world that is teeming with life.[1]

Read these words again. In time they will give you a spark of hope.

48

Share Your Heart

O LORD, do not rebuke me in your anger or discipline me in your wrath. Be merciful to me, LORD, for I am faint: O LORD, heal me, for my bones are in agony. My soul is in anguish. How long, O LORD, how long? Turn, O LORD, and deliver me; save me because of your unfailing love. No one remembers you when he is dead. Who praises you from the grave? I am worn out from groaning; all night long I flood my bed with weeping and drench my couch with tears. My eyes grow weak with sorrow; they fail because of all my foes. Away from me, all you who do evil, for the LORD has heard my weeping. The LORD has heard my cry for mercy; the LORD accepts my prayer (Psalm 6:1-9).

One thing I love about the Bible is its brutal honesty. It never shrinks from telling the truth, even if unlovely or downright ugly. And because of the uncompromising honesty, it has the power to set us on a healing track. As Jesus himself said, "You will know the truth, and the truth will set you free" (John 8:32).

One of the truths the Bible tells us is we are just as fragile emotionally as we are physically. Some of us don't like to hear that. It's probably easier for most people to accept physical frailty than it is to admit emotional frailty.

In the midst of great physical suffering, it is important not to ignore the emotional side of suffering. The advice "Just suck it up" does not work. Our mental state enormously affects our physical state. Fears, grief, and anger all need to be expressed in order to bring physical healing. When bottled up inside, these emotions will destroy us. God knows what we're feeling anyway, so why try to hide it?

King David, especially, poured out his heart to God. He was absolutely unafraid of bringing all his emotions into the open. Name an emotion, and you can probably find it in one of David's psalms.

> *Fear?* "When I am afraid, I will trust in you" (Psalm 56:3).
>
> *Weakness?* "Be merciful to me, LORD, for I am faint" (Psalm 6:2).
>
> *Anguish?* "My soul is in anguish" (Psalm 6:3).
>
> *Impatience?* "How long, O LORD, how long?" (Psalm 6:3).
>
> *Grief?* "All night long I flood my bed with weeping and drench my couch with tears" (Psalm 6:6).
>
> *Sorrow?* "My eyes grow weak with sorrow" (Psalm 6:7).

Note that all of these examples (except for the first one) are from a single psalm! David was unashamed to pour out his heart to God in all its emotional intensity and even fury. And note something else, too: God saw fit to put these emotional psalms into Holy Scripture. Why? Because he couldn't find anything more doctrinally correct to include and he had to put in something? Hardly. God wants us to be truthful with him, and the psalms are among the most transparent human records in existence. They prove that it is possible to be both godly and honest.

We are not being honest when we're churning inside and yet go to God in prayer in our best King James vocabulary, trying to sound unperturbed and unruffled and all righteous and holy. That's phony. Who are we trying to fool, trying to sound so righteous before a holy and all-knowing God? He knows exactly what's going on inside us, even if we won't admit it. In those times, we need to follow David's example and tell God exactly how we feel, even though we risk saying wrong things. God invites us to share our hearts with him, to confess our sins and our fears and our insecurities and our worries, and then to ask him to change our hearts.[1]

49

Tears Are a Messenger

We hear about survivors all the time. They're front-page copy for newspapers or they appear in articles in *Reader's Digest*. We want to know, "How did they do that?" We also want to know how people survive the losses and crises of life. One common characteristic is showing their feelings—including *hurt* and *anger*. They don't bottle up their hurt feelings, nor do they complain and force their discomfort on others. They talk, they share, and they cry. Oh, how they cry! Tears are God's gift, especially at times like these.

When words fail, tears are the messenger. Tears are God's gift to all of us to release our feelings. When Jesus arrived in Bethany following the death of Lazarus, he wept (John 11:35). And so will we. Author Ken Gire describes the value of tears:

> The closest communion with God comes, I believe, through the sacrament of tears. Just as grapes are crushed to make wine and grain to make bread, so the elements of this sacrament come from the crushing experiences of life.
>
> And sometimes the crushing starts early.
>
> One day your dog doesn't come home and you go calling for it. Another day passes, and you go looking for it. And on the third day when you're looking for it,

you find its stiff body on the side of a well-trafficked street, and you bundle it up, carry it off, dig a hole in the backyard, and you bury it with a rock as a tombstone and tears as a eulogy.

Or someone at school dies from a cerebral hemorrhage, or several someones in a sudden car wreck.

Or you learn from the orthopedic doctor that you can no longer play the sport you have loved for half of your still very young life, and maybe it's not the thing that should bring tears, but it does.

Or a grandparent dies. A grandparent who loved you and teased you and hugged you and brought "a little something for you" every time she came to visit. And now there's a freshly dug hole in the backyard of your heart.

Or a parent dies, and now the whole backyard is one big hole.

Or a marriage ends between two people you thought would be the last to break up, and besides the grief you feel, you sense the mortar of life loosening a little and the unsettling feeling that if it could happen to them, it could happen to anyone, even to you....[1]

I have learned that if you follow your tears, you will find your heart. If you find your heart, you will find what is dear to God. And if you find what is dear to God, you will find the answers to how you should live your life.[2]

When our tears come, instead of feeling bad for shedding them or apologizing for them, we can treasure their value. They're a gift from God.

$\mathcal{A}$ Constant Source of Comfort

$\sim$

Comfort comes from places you expect, as well as those you least expect. It could be the words of a friend or even your friend's silent presence. It could be a look, a thumb's up, or a hug. It could be your cat leaping into your lap or your dog laying his chin on your leg.

There is something, however, that is a constant source of comfort—the words of God. There is a way his words will stick with you and bring the comfort you're seeking. Read the words of Scripture aloud. For example, here is Psalm 46:1-6:

> God is our Refuge and Strength [mighty *and* impenetrable to temptation], a very present *and* well-proved help in trouble. Therefore we will not fear, though the earth should change and though the mountains be shaken into the midst of the seas, Though its waters roar and foam, though the mountains tremble at its swelling and tumult. Selah [pause, and calmly think of that]! There is a river whose streams shall make glad the city of God, the holy place of the tabernacles of the Most High. God is in the midst of her, she shall not be moved; God will help her right early [at the dawn of the morning]. The nations raged, the

kingdoms tottered *and* were moved; He uttered His voice, the earth melted (AMP).

What helps if you lost a Christian loved one, is to insert his or her name into your reading. For example, "There is a river whose stream shall make glad the city of God including [name of the one you lost] who lives there—the holy place of the tabernacle of the Most High."

If you read this passage several times a day, in a short while, it would be memorized. There are many passages you can read to give you hope and encouragement about where your loved one is, as well as provide hope for your journey of grief.

Read these passages morning and evening, and let their truths sink into your life:

> He heals the brokenhearted and binds up their wounds [curing their pains and their sorrows] (Psalm 147:3 AMP).

> I cried out to the LORD in my suffering, and he heard me. He set me free from all my fears (Psalm 34:6 NLT).

> For You have delivered my life from death, my eyes from tears, and my feet from stumbling *and* falling. I will walk before the Lord in the land of the living (Psalm 116:8-9 AMP).

> Then maidens will dance and be glad, young men and old as well, I will turn their mourning into gladness; I will give them comfort and joy instead of sorrow (Jeremiah 31:13).

> You will grieve but your grief will turn to joy (John 16:20).

What verses bring comfort to you? Read the psalms. Read them aloud. When you pray—no matter the content—pray out loud.

Your prayers are important to you and to God. "I love the Lord because he hears and answers my prayers. Because he bends down and listens, I will pray as long as I have breath!" (Psalm 116:1-2 NLT).

51

It's All Right
to Ask Why

There's a man in the Old Testament who had a difficult life, not just for a few months or years, but for decades. What he had to say to the people he lived with wasn't very pleasant nor was it accepted. They didn't want to hear his pleas to turn to God. He pleaded with them for almost 40 years, and then they were taken captive. He kept at it even when he wanted to give up. He wrote:

> I have become a laughingstock all day long....
> But if I say, "I will not remember (God)
> Or speak anymore in His name,"
> Then in my heart it becomes like a burning fire
> Shut up in my bones;
> And I am weary of holding it in,
> And I cannot endure it
> (Jeremiah 20:7,9 NASB).

Jeremiah was very honest. He let God know he was upset and unhappy. He hadn't asked for his job as a prophet. He didn't want it, and now he was suffering because of it. He felt God wasn't honest with him. This is what he said:

> O LORD, You have deceived me....
> Everyone mocks me.
> For each time I speak, I cry aloud;
> I proclaim violence and destruction,
> Because for me the word of the LORD has resulted
> In reproach and derision all day long
> (Jeremiah 20:7-8 NASB).

Jeremiah was so upset he cursed the day he was born, asking:

> Why did I ever come forth from the womb
> To look on trouble and sorrow,
> So that my days have been spent in shame?
> (Jeremiah 20:18 NASB).

Listen to what Ruth Graham said about life:

> When life becomes burdensome and all but impossible to bear, often the only question we have to ask is, "Why?" I have heard people say, "You can't ask God why." Yes we can. We can ask God why. We're in good company when we ask. Jeremiah asked God why. Many heroes of the faith have asked God why.

Asking why does not mean we have lost our faith. As I came to understand, asking why can be, rather, a sign of faith. When we ask why, we are asserting our desire to dialogue with the God in whom we have put a measure of trust. We expect he is listening and believe he is the source of the answers.

But won't we offend God if we ask why? Won't we make him angry? God is not threatened by our emotions. He is not shaken by our "why?" He did not strike Jeremiah down for expressing frustration and despair. God works with honesty. He invites honesty. We cannot throw anything at God that he hasn't heard before. He is bigger than our feelings, thoughts, and perceptions.

At the same time, as we express ourselves to God, we must keep our hearts soft and open to him. For all of his distress, Jeremiah remained determined to obey God, no matter what the cost. He fussed, argued, and wrestled with God, but his heart was submitted to God. He trusted God even as he was questioning him.

Ultimately, Jeremiah did not allow himself to become bitter. In fact, in the midst of his suffering Jeremiah was able to pen some of the most beautiful lines about God in all of Scripture. He wrote:

> It is of the LORD's mercies that we are not consumed, because his compassions fail not.
> They are new every morning: great is thy faithfulness.
> The LORD is my portion, saith my soul; therefore will I hope in him (Lamentations 3:22-24 KJV).

Recall the context in which Jeremiah lived, and then imagine him praying these words. Did he learn God's faithfulness while trapped at the bottom of the well? Did he know God's loving-kindness while wearing the yoke around his neck? Was he looking out over the remains of his city, now burned to the ground, when he recognized—and could declare—the goodness of God? Whatever our range of emotions, whatever our view of the circumstances unfolding around us, may we, like Jeremiah, keep our hearts open to God's faithfulness.[1]

52

Keeping Focus
in the Storm

$\sim$

What are you looking at right now? Had you ever thought of what you would spend your time focusing upon during times of difficulty? If you're like most of us, you may have a radar lock on the problem or loss that you're struggling with. It could be you're hoping that if you concentrate on it enough, it will go away. But it won't. It will loom bigger in your mind. It grows in size and intensity. The relief and comfort you're looking for becomes more elusive. The Scriptures tell a story that illustrates this:

> Immediately Jesus made the disciples get into the boat and go on ahead of him to the other side, while he dismissed the crowd. After he had dismissed them, he went up on a mountainside by himself to pray. When evening came, he was there alone, but the boat was already a considerable distance from land, buffeted by the waves because the wind was against it. During the fourth watch of the night Jesus went out to them, walking on the lake. When the disciples saw him walking on the lake, they were terrified. "It's a ghost," they said, and cried out in fear.
>
> But Jesus immediately said to them, "Take courage! It is I. Don't be afraid."

"Lord, if it's you," Peter replied, "tell me to come to you on the water."

"Come," he said.

Then Peter got down out of the boat, walked on the water and came toward Jesus. But when he saw the wind, he was afraid and, beginning to sink, cried out, "Lord, save me!" (Matthew 14:22-30).

Peter created a problem because he took his eyes off Jesus and looked at the waves. And the result was obvious—he began to sink. When we look at just the problem, we can't see the solution. When we look at just our loss and grief, we have difficulty seeing hope in the future. We miss out on the comfort that is there, ready for the asking. We begin to think it isn't available. Listen to the comforting words of Dr. Charles Stanley,

> The God of all comfort can lovingly touch all heartache, despair, darkness, pain, evil, and desperation. Your tribulations are severe. Your path is hard. Your conditions are bleak. Your outlook is dim. But the God of all comfort—the God who Himself has suffered indescribably at the hands of people—will aid you, encourage you, strengthen you, and guide you.
>
> Because Christ has experienced the ridicule and rejection of people and now stands as the Great High Priest, the throne of grace beckons every believer.
>
> In the heat of the fight—the Light of Life is with you.
>
> In the midst of the storm—the Prince of Peace is your steadfast guide.
>
> In the bottom of the pit—the Chief Cornerstone is your rock.
>
> If you hurt, let the healing love of Jesus Christ sustain you. He longs to comfort and encourage you with His presence, His promises, His people, and His power.

The God of all comfort will not let you go over the edge or sink beneath the mire. He will come instantly to your aid as you call on His name.

One day He will use you to personally carry His comfort to the ailing heart of another—transforming your trouble into His healing balm.

Lord, thank you that in the heat of the fight, your Light is with me. Thank you that in the midst of the storm, the Prince of Peace is my guide, in the bottom of the pit, O God, the Chief Cornerstone is my rock.[1]

53

What Will You Write?

They go around and around in your mind—images, words, feelings, and thoughts. If you could find the off button, you would push it. The feelings we experience in grief play over and over again like a stuck recording. They're looking for some form of expression, and you're probably searching for someone to drain them so your mind and heart can rest.

In pain, grief, or affliction, it often helps to write our feelings…not just feel them. Putting words on paper seems to free our feelings from the lonely prison of our souls. It was C.S. Lewis who wrote:

> Her absence is like the sky spread over everything…. No one ever told me that grief felt so like fear. I am not afraid, but the sensation is like being afraid. The same fluttering in the stomach, the same restlessness, the yawning. I keep on swallowing.

It was William Armstrong who wrote:

> Back in the house I moved on leaden feet from chore to chore.

Ada Campbell Rose wrote:

The mantle of grief falls on every hour of the day and covers me while I sleep. Will it ever go away?

King David wrote:

Even when walking through the dark valley of death I will not be afraid, for you are close beside me, guarding, guiding all the way (Psalm 23:4 TLB).

The apostle Paul wrote:

I will say this: because these experiences I had were so tremendous, God was afraid I might be puffed up by them; so I was given a physical condition which has been a thorn in my flesh, a messenger from Satan to hurt and bother me, and prick my pride. Three different times I begged God to make me well again.

Each time he said, "No. But I am with you; that is all you need. My power shows up best in weak people." Now I am glad to boast about how weak I am; I am glad to be a living demonstration of Christ's power, instead of showing off my own power and abilities. Since I know it is all for Christ's good, I am quite happy about "the thorn," and about insults and hardships, persecutions and difficulties; for when I am weak, then I am strong—the less I have, the more I depend on him (2 Corinthians 12:7-10 TLB).

George Matheson wrote:

My God, I have never thanked Thee for my thorns. I have thanked Thee a thousand times for my *roses*, but not once for my *thorns*. I have been looking forward to a world where I shall get compensation for my cross: but I have never thought of my cross as itself a present glory. Teach me the glory of my cross: teach me the

value of my thorn. Show me that I have climbed to
Thee by the path of pain. Show me that my tears have
made my rainbow.

As you feel the stinging thorns of pain today, what do *you*
write? *Nothing?* Healing stands with folded arms waiting to read
your words.[1]

54

*P*rayers for Help

For years now, part of what I do is read prayers written by others. William Barclay has been one of my favorite writers. The following two prayers may reflect some of what you may be experiencing. Read them aloud, then go back and think through what the various sentences are saying:

> O God, our Father, you alone can enable us to accept
>   and to obey your commandments and to do your
>   will.
> Increase our faith.
> Help us,
>   To trust you when the skies are dark;
>   To accept that which we cannot understand;
>   To be quite sure that all things can work together for
>   good to those who love you.
> Increase our hope.
> Give us,
>   The hope which has seen things at their worst,
>   and which refuses to despair;
>   The hope that is able to fail,
>   and yet to try again;
>   The hope which can accept disappointment,
>   and yet not abandon hope.
> Increase our love.

Help us,
> To love our fellow men and women, as you love
> them;
> To love you as you have first loved us;
> To love loyalty to our Lord above all things.

Help us so to love you that your commandments will never be a weariness and a burden to us, but that it will be a joy for us to obey them, so that in obedience to you we may find our perfect freedom, and in doing your will our peace.

So grant us,
> To fight the good fight;
> To run the straight race;
> To keep the faith,
> > that we may win the glory and the crown.

Hear these our prayers for your love's sake. Amen.[1]

O God, you are our refuge.
> When we are exhausted by life's efforts;
> When we are bewildered by life's problems;
> When we are wounded by life's sorrows;
> > We come for refuge to you.

O God, you are our strength.
> When our tasks are beyond our powers;
> When our temptations are too strong for us;
> When duty calls for more than we have to give to it;
> > We come for strength to you.

O God, it is from you that all goodness comes.
> It is from you that our ideals come;
> It is from you that there comes to us
> > the spur of high desire and the restraint of con-
> > science.
> It is from you that there has come the strength
> > to resist any temptation,
> > and to do any good thing.

And now as we pray to you,

Help us to believe in your love,
    so that we may be certain
    that you will hear our prayer;
Help us to believe in your power,
    so that we may be certain
    that you are able to do for us
    above all that we ask or think;
Help us to believe in your wisdom,
    so that we may be certain
    that you will answer,
    not as our ignorance asks,
    but as your perfect wisdom knows best.
All this we ask through Jesus Christ our Lord.
    Amen.[2]

55

$\mathcal{Y}$ou Can Survive, Too

Survivors say, "I can face the challenge of life and handle the stress and crises of life without denying their existence or giving up." I especially like this last attitude of a survivor. It's not just what happens to us; it's how we respond to what happens to us that's so important. It's the ability to take James 1:2-3 and apply it to our lives: "Consider it pure joy, my brothers, whenever you face trials of many kinds, because you know the testing of your faith develops perseverance." Remember, a survivor is a person who makes sense out of what happens to him. Never, never let your hand slip off of your hope.[1]

A friend of mine was afflicted by multiple sclerosis. Dave was a survivor. During the beginning years of his disease, he experienced the pain of divorce as well. In 1990, when he was still somewhat ambulatory, he remarried a woman 14 years younger. In preparation for their life together with a disease that would become progressively worse, they both attended several national conferences on multiple sclerosis to learn as much as they could about what to expect in the future. Lisa began cooking his specialized diet even before their marriage. They discussed issues they thought they would face in the future, including the age factor, who would eventually support the family, whether or not to have children.

They have two children, and Dave stayed at home because he

had to retire on disability from his work. Lisa taught school until noon and then returned home. I asked Dave, "How have you made it? How do you go on?" This is what he told me:

> First of all, it is my relationship with the Lord. My faith in Him has sustained me. Then it's been Lisa. In our wedding vows she pledged to be my hands and feet. And more and more she's doing this. I've learned to make adjustments in my life for what I could no longer do. It was difficult to respond to letters and E-mail with my computer. So I was able to obtain a voice-activated computer, and I'm able to be as verbal as ever in my responses.
>
> Another factor has been the memorizing of God's Word. I recite the verses out loud, which strengthens my mouth muscles. With MS, your speech tends to get sloppy, and doing this helps to keep this from occurring. You lose so many abilities as it is with MS. Each time you lose one you have to fight the tendency to give up on everything. When each ability goes you have to grieve over that loss just like you did before. You never finish the process of grieving throughout this. But memorizing God's Word gives you the inner strength and confidence as well as depending upon the Lord.

Do you see all the factors involved in this man's survival? Dave's faith in God and his reliance upon others, especially his wife, were strong factors in overcoming his disabilities. Dave wouldn't give up. He moved ahead with his life with a new family, making adjustments, discovering new ways to function, relying upon God's Word, and facing his losses by grieving over them. This is what it takes to move on.

I like the following prayer by Chuck Swindoll. I encourage you to make it yours:

It's not often, Father, that we make such a statement, but today we thank You for the injustices that have crippled us and broken us and crushed us. We want to express our appreciation for the things that have brought us to the place of submission.

We express our gratitude for the things You have taught us through blindness and loss and paralysis; for growth through broken dreams, dissolved partnerships, illness and sadness; for the character development through insecurity, failure, and even divorce. We see the storm, but we are beginning to see You beyond the storm. How essential is our attitude!

Thank You especially for helping us to conquer our cynicism.

I pray for those in these and a hundred other categories, that we may be able to go beyond them and find in Jesus Christ the strength to go on, especially for those who, only a few moments ago, had just about decided to give up. I pray that they will rather give it all to You in full surrender.

In the strong name of Jesus Christ, the Conqueror, I pray. Amen.[2]

Saying Goodbye to Grief

I feel disoriented. I can't seem to get my bearings." That's what many say, but the disorientation connected with your grief will diminish. How will you know that it's about over? Several signs will indicate that you are adjusting and recovering.

One of the first signs is a sense of release. It's a turning about in the focus of your thinking. Instead of your thoughts being locked onto the memories of your loved one or wondering what he (she) would be thinking or doing, it's more of thinking about living your own life now and for the future. You reach out more and feel as though you're living life. As one woman said, "My sorrow now feels less like an oppressive weight, more…like a treasured possession. I can take it out and ponder it, then put it safely and carefully away."

Another indication is the renewal of your energy. The fatigue begins to lift. Activities that you wanted to engage in before you can now respond to.

A third change is your capability of having better judgment. It usually takes longer for this to occur than most expect. Decision-making involves concentration, and those in grief find this difficult. Thoughts are jumbled and staying focused is a challenge.[1] But as you recover it will become easier to make decisions.

Many ask for a specific road map for their recovery. Their questions are really, What do I do to recover and how will I know that I'm getting there? Here are some guidelines that may help:

- You are able to handle the finality of the death.

- You can review pleasant as well as unpleasant memories.

- You can choose to spend time alone and enjoy it.

- You can go somewhere without crying most of the time.

- You are beginning to look forward to holidays.

- You are able to help others in a similar situation.

- You're able to listen to your loved one's music without pain.

- You can sit through a worship service without crying.

- You can laugh at a joke.

- Your eating, sleeping, and exercise patterns are returning to what they were before the death.

- You can concentrate on reading or watching TV.

- You're no longer tired.

- You can find something to be thankful for.

- You are beginning to build new relationships.

- You are beginning to experience life again.

- You are patient with yourself when you experience a "grief spasm" again.

- You are beginning to discover new personal growth from your grief.[2]

Recovery involves many elements such as diet, exercise, rest, and sleep. Recovery from loss is like having to get off the main highway every so many miles because the main route is under construction. The road signs reroute you through little towns you hadn't expected to visit and over bumpy roads you hadn't wanted to bounce around on. You are basically traveling in the appropriate direction. On the map, however, the course you are following has the look of shark's teeth instead of a straight line. Although you are gradually getting there, you sometimes doubt that you will ever meet up with the finished highway. There is a finished highway in your future. You won't know when or where, but it is there. You will discover a greater sense of resilience when you know in advance what you will experience and that you're normal in your response.[3]

As you continue remembering, the pain will subside. Right now it may be shouting, but someday it will whisper. The ache in your heart will go away. You may not think this possible at this point in your life, but hearing these words can make this time in your life more bearable. If you are a Christian, your grief is different. It's infused with hope. The foundation for this hope is found in the death and resurrection of Jesus Christ. "He is the Lord over every loss and every heartache. He is the Lord of all comfort and mercy. He is the Lord of resurrection, restoration, and regeneration. He is the Lord of life."[4]

Hope will return to replace the despair. The dust of drought and dark clouds will change. There will be a smile instead of a frown, a calmness instead of being on edge. When? When you've gone through your grief and fulfilled your time. Knowing how long doesn't make it easier. As the writers said, "There is a time for everything, and a season for every activity under heaven...a time to weep and a time to laugh, a time to mourn and a time to dance" (Ecclesiastes 3:1,4). "The LORD will be your everlasting light, and your days of sorrow will end" (Isaiah 60:20).[5]

The Promise of Heaven

Heaven. Do you ever think about it or wonder about it? It seems so distant, and yet it's not. It's a place where we will experience the security of being sheltered by God. It's a place where we will experience eternal satisfaction.

> Never again will they hunger;
>   never again will they thirst.
> The sun will not beat upon them,
>   nor any scorching heat (Revelation 7:16).

The concerns that consume so much of our time and energy on earth will be all met in heaven. What we will experience instead is the direct provision of the Shepherd Jesus himself.

> For the Lamb at the center of the throne
>   will be their shepherd;
> he will lead them to springs of living water.
> And God will wipe away every tear
>   from their eyes (Revelation 7:17).

Heaven sets us free from all the things that weigh upon our minds at the present time. Tears of sorrow or remorse or pain or loss are a regular part of life now but never in heaven.

A pastor talked about heaven and described it in a very different way. He called it "Living Now in Light of the Not Yet." This is what he said:

> I'm fascinated by the fact that the explanation of heaven's joys was given to John by one of the elders around God's throne. This wasn't an angel's perspective or even God's personal declaration. These words came from someone who had experienced heaven personally as a redeemed human being. The elder knew what it was like to be sheltered under the protective tent of God. He knew the fulfillment of serving God as a priest. He had come to the springs of living water and been deeply satisfied. He knew what it was like to have God "wipe away every tear."
>
> I think this phrase means far more than that we will never cry again. I think it means that in heaven we will come to understand *why* we cried so many tears here on earth. We will see the pattern of our lives from God's perspective, and we will see that everything God did was very good. We will finally see how God was working all things together for our good and for his glory. Right now our understanding of what God is doing is limited and even distorted by our own selfishness. We don't begin to comprehend why God would allow sickness to strike us or a crippling disease to afflict someone we love. We cry stinging tears over a child who seems to be far from the Lord, but we can't see what God is doing in that child's life to bring him back to him. But someday we will see the design that God is weaving, and even the tears we've cried here will be tenderly wiped away.
>
> A friend of mine carries a piece of a jigsaw puzzle around in his pocket. The picture is worn off and the edges are frayed, but he carries it as a constant reminder

of how God works in his life. At a particularly difficult time in my friend's life, when he struggled with an out-of-control child and a collapsing business, his wife suggested that they put a jigsaw puzzle together over a holiday weekend. As they worked on the puzzle, they had the opportunity to talk about the issues that pressed so heavily on their hearts. When the puzzle was finished and the picture emerged, the wife pulled one piece from the center of the puzzle. "This piece is all you see of the puzzle of your life today," she said. "Only God sees the finished picture." The worn-out puzzle piece in his pocket is a constant reminder that God is working in his life, even when he cannot see how all the pieces fit together.

God knows what you are struggling with right now. If you are his child, that pain or loss is just one piece in God's plan—and it may be the piece that comes from the focal point of the finished design. God does not promise to explain our trials. He just asks us to trust him, to believe that he really is in control and that he has not abandoned us. But someday the picture he is putting together will be revealed in all its complexity and beauty. When that happens, the joy we will experience in the goodness of God will wipe out all the pain we feel right now.[1]

So, when you need comfort, what could be more comforting than realizing you're not alone? God is at work even when you wonder, "Where is he?" And there is a place reserved just for you and everyone else who knows Jesus as Lord and Savior of his or her life.

Notes

Two

1. David Jeremiah, *A Bend in the Road* (Nashville: Word, 2000), pp. 66-74, adapted.

2. Eugene Peterson, *A Long Obedience in the Same Direction* (Downer's Grove, IL: InterVarsity Press, 1980), pp. 40-41.

Three

1. Raymond R. Mitsch and Lynn Brookside, *Grieving the Loss of Someone You Love* (Ventura, CA: Gospel Light/Regal Books, 2004), pp. 40-42. Used by permission.

Four

1. Mel Lawrenz and Daniel Green, *Life After Grief* (Grand Rapids, MI: Baker Books, 1995), pp. 119-22, adapted.

Five

1. Pamela and Richard Kennedy, *Suffering in Slow Motion* (Ventura, CA: Regal Books, 2003), p. 83, adapted.

Six

1. Pamela and Richard Kennedy, *Suffering in Slow Motion* (Ventura, CA: Regal Books, 2003), p. 83, adapted.

2. Ibid., pp. 78-80, adapted.

3. Lewis Smedes, *How Can It Be All Right When Everything Is All Wrong?* (San Francisco: Harper & Row, 1982), p. 128.

Seven

1. Susan J. Zonnebelt-Smeenge, RN, Ed.D, and Robert C. DeVries, D.Min, Ph.D., *Getting to the Other Side of Grief* (Grand Rapids, MI: Baker Books, 1998), pp. 56-60, adapted. Used by permission.

2. Ibid, p. 61.

Eight

1. Susan J. Zonnebelt-Smeenge, RN, Ed.D, and Robert C. DeVries, D.Min, Ph.D., *Getting to the Other Side of Grief* (Grand Rapids, MI: Baker Books, 1998, pp. 18-19, 214, adapted. Used by permission.

2. Robert DeVries in ibid., quoted with partial adaptation, pp. 215-16. Used by permission.

Ten

1. William Barclay, *A Barclay Prayer Book* (Philadelphia: Trinity Press, Inc., 1990), pp. 42-43.

Eleven

1. Charles Swindoll, *Growing Strong in the Seasons of Life* (Portland, OR: Multnomah Press, 1983), pp. 135-36, adapted.

Thirteen

1. Wayne Monbleau, *You Don't Find Water on the Mountaintop* (Grand Rapids, MI: Fleming H. Revell, 1996), pp. 36-41, adapted.

Fourteen

1. Dr. Cyne Barber and Sharalee Aspenboder, *Through the Valley of Tears* (Old Tappan, NJ: Fleming H. Revell, 1987), pp. 93-94.

Fifteen

1. C.S. Lewis, *Mere Christianity* (New York: Macmillan, 1943), p. 54.

2. Gerry Sittser, *When God Doesn't Answer Your Prayer* (Grand Rapids, MI: Zondervan, 2003), p. 154.

Sixteen

1. Joni Earickson Tada and Steven Estes, *When God Weeps* (Grand Rapids, MI: Zondervan, 1997), pp. 199-201, adapted. Used by permission.

Seventeen

1. In Harold Ivan Smith, *Grievers Ask* (Minneapolis: Augsburg Books, 2004), p. 8, adapted.

2. Ibid., pp. 1-15, adapted.

3. Alan D. Wolfelt, "Lecture" (Olathe, KS), February 17, 1999.

Eighteen

1. David Jeremiah, *A Bend in the Road* (Nashville: Word, 2000), pp. 46-48, adapted.

Nineteen

1. Tommy Walker, *He Knows My Name* (Ventura, CA: Gospel Light/Regal Books, 2004), pp. 88-91. Used by permission.

Twenty

1. Philip Yancey, *Disappointment with God* (Grand Rapids, MI: Zondervan, 1988), p. 284.

2. Richard Foster, *Prayers from the Heart* (New York: HarperCollins, 1994).

Twenty-Two

1. Zig Zigler, *Confessions of a Grieving Christian* (Nashville: Thomas Nelson Publishers, 1998), pp. 71-73. Used by permission.

Twenty-Three

1. Joanne T. Jozefowski, *The Phoenix Phenomenon* (Northvale, NJ: Ransom, 1999), p. 17.

2. Raymond R. Mitsch and Lynn Brookside, *Grieving the Loss of Someone You Love* (Ann Arbor, MI: Servant Publications, 1993), pp. 21-23, adapted.

Twenty-Four

1. Lilly Singer, Margaret Sirot, and Susan Rodd, *Beyond Loss* (New York: E.P. Dutton, 1988), p. 62.

2. Therese A. Rando, *Grieving: How to Go on Living When Someone You Love Dies* (Lexington, MA: Lexington Books, 1988), pp. 11-12, adapted.

3. Ibid., pp. 18-19, adapted.

4. Bob Deits, *Life After Loss* (Tucson, AZ: Fisher Books, 1988), p. 28, adapted.

5. James Froehlich, O.F.M. Cap, in a paper written for the Pastoral Helping Relationship graduate course at Loyola College (Baltimore: 1984).

Twenty-Five

1. Max Lucado, *In the Eye of the Storm* (Dallas: Word, Inc., 1991), pp. 105-06.

2. Lewis Smedes, *How Can It Be All Right When Everything Is All Wrong?* (San Francisco: Harper & Row, 1982), pp. 55-56.

Twenty-Six

1. Larry Richards, *When It Hurts Too Much to Wait* (Dallas: Word, Inc., 1985), pp. 67-68.

Twenty-Seven

1. Max Lucado, *The Applause of Heaven* (Dallas: Word, Inc., 1990), pp. 186-87.

2. Ibid., p. 190.

Twenty-Eight

1. Rainer Maria Rilke, *Letters to a Young Poet* (Mineola, NY: Dover Publications, 2002).

2. Ted Loder, *Guerillas of Grace* (Philadelphia: Innisfree Press, 1984).

Twenty-Nine

1. Frederick Buechner, *A Room Called Remember* (New York: Harper & Row, 1984), p. 4.

2. Michael Lewing, *A Common Prayer.*

Thirty

1. Billy Sprague, *Letter to a Grieving Heart* (Eugene, OR: Harvest House, 2001), p. 39. Used by permission.

2. Ibid., p. 16.

Thirty-One

1. Billy Sprague, *Letters to a Grieving Heart* (Eugene, OR: Harvest House, 2001), pp. 62-63. Used by permission.

Thirty-Two

1. Ann Kaiser Stearns, *Coming Back* (New York: Ballantine, 1988), p. 172.

2. David W. Wiersbe, *Gone but Not Lost* (Grand Rapids, MI: Baker, 1992), p. 55.

Thirty-Three

1. Ann Weems, *Psalms of Lament* (Louisville: Westminster John Knox Press, 1995), pp. 55-56. Used by permission.

Thirty-Four

1. "And the Father Will Dance," lyrics adapted from Zephaniah 3:14,17 and Psalm 54:2,4. Arranged by Mark Hayes.

2. John Piper, *The Pleasures of God* (Portland, OR: Multnomah Press, 1991), p. 188.

Thirty-Five

1. Joyce Landorf, *Mourning Song* (Old Tappan, NJ: Fleming H. Revell, 1974), pp. 150-51.

Thirty-Six

1. Shirley Inrau, "Learning with a Dying Mother," *Confident Living* (December 1987), pp. 20-22.

Thirty-Seven

1. Dwight Carlson, *When Life Isn't Fair* (Eugene, OR: Harvest House Publishers, 1989), p. 52.

2. Harold Kushner, *When Bad Things Happen to Good People* (New York: Avon Books, 1981), p. 121.

Thirty-Eight

1. *The Book of Common Prayer* (New York: Seabury, 1979), p. 323.

2. *The Oxford Book of Prayers* (Oxford: Oxford University Press, 1985), p. 333.

Thirty-Nine

1. Zig Zigler, *Confessions of a Grieving Christian* (Nashville: Thomas Nelson Publishers, 1998), pp. 3-7, adapted.

Forty

1. Joyce Rupp, *Praying Our Goodbyes* (New York: Ivy Books, 1988), pp. 6-7.

2. Raymond Mitsch and Lynn Brookside, *Grieving the Loss of Someone You Love* (Ventura, CA: Regal Books, 1993, pp. 146-47, adapted.

Forty-One

1. Ron Mehl, *God Works the Night Shift* (Sisters, OR: Multnomah Books, 1994), p. 18.

2. Ibid., pp. 20-21.

Forty-Two

1. William Barclay, *Prayers for Help and Healing* (Minneapolis: Augsburg Press, 1968), p. 43.

Forty-Four

1. Susan Zonnebelt-Smeenge and Robert DeVries, *Living Fully in the Shadow of Death* (Grand Rapids, MI: Baker Books, 2004), p. 62.

Forty-Five

1. Dr. Jerry Jones, *Beyond the Storm* (West Monroe, LA: Howard Publishing Co., 1997), pp. 223-25, adapted.

Forty-Seven

1. Gerald L. Sittser, *A Grace Disguised* (Grand Rapids, MI: Zondervan, 1995), pp. 40, 65. Used by permission.

Forty-Eight

1. Dave and Jan Dravecky, *Do Not Lose Heart* (Grand Rapids, MI: Zondervan, 1998), pp. 45-46, adapted.

Forty-Nine

1. Ken Gire, *Windows of the Soul* (Grand Rapids, MI: Zondervan, 1996), pp. 193-94.

2. Ibid., p. 195.

Fifty-One

1. Ruth Graham, *In Every Pew Sits a Broken Heart* (Grand Rapids, MI: Zondervan, 2004), pp. 39-40, adapted.

Fifty-Two

1. Charles Stanley, *Enter His Gates* (Nashville: Thomas Nelson, 1998), p. 77.

Fifty-Three

1. Chuck Swindoll, *Come Before Winter* (Portland, OR: Multnomah Press, 1985), pp. 313-14.

Fifty-Four

1. William Barclay, *A Barclay Prayer Book* (Philadelphia: Trinity Press International, 1963), pp. 116-17.

2. Ibid., pp. 134-35.

Fifty-Five

1. Ann Kaiser Stearns, *Coming Back* (New York: Random House, 1988), pp. 58-179, adapted.

2. Charles Swindoll, *Living on the Ragged Edge* (Nashville: Thomas Nelson/W Publishing, 1990).

Fifty-Six

1. Glen W. Davidson, *Understanding Mourning* (Minneapolis: Augsburg Publishing House, 1984), pp. 78-80, adapted.

2. Helen Fitzgerald, *The Mourning Handbook* (New York: Simon & Schuster, 1994), pp. 249-50, adapted.

3. Ann Kaiser Stearns, *Coming Back* (New York: Random House, 1988), pp. 85-86.

4. Claire Cloninger, *Postcards for Those That Hurt* (Dallas: Word Publishing, 1995), p. 55.

5. Raymond R. Mitsch and Lynn Brookside, *Grieving the Loss of Someone You Love* (Ann Arbor, MI: Servant Publications, 1993), pp. 177-78, adapted.

Fifty-Seven

1. Douglas Connelly, *The Promises of Heaven* (Downer's Grove, IL: Inter-Varsity Press, 2000), pp. 43-45. Used by permission.

FROM TODDLERS TO TEENS
Helping Your
Kids Deal with
ANGER,
FEAR, and
SADNESS

H. NORMAN WRIGHT

Helping Your Kids Deal with Anger, Fear, and Sadness

No parent likes to see their child struggle, especially with dark emotions like anger, fear, and depression. Family counselor and bestselling author Norm Wright addresses these emotional issues in a compassionate, family-friendly way that will help parents to communicate more freely with their children.

Included in this interactive parenting manual are conversational guidelines and learning activities for children that encourage them to work through these difficult emotions. Parents will gain keen insights into the cause of these intense moods and develop sound principles in dealing effectively with them.

Biblically based and solution-oriented, *Helping Your Kids Deal with Anger, Fear, and Depression* is a must-have for parents, Sunday school teachers, ministers, and family counselors.

Other Books
by H. Norman Wright

101 Questions to Ask Before You Get Engaged

After You Say "I Do"

After You Say "I Do" Devotional

Before You Say "I Do"®

Before You Say "I Do"® Devotional

Finding Your Perfect Mate

A Friend Like No Other

*Helping Your Kids Deal with
Anger, Fear, and Sadness*

The Purrfect Companion

Quiet Times for Couples

Winning Over Your Emotions

Would You Like to Host a Seminar with H. Norman Wright?

We have openings available for a few area-wide, one-day seminars with Norman Wright as seminar leader!

GRIEF RECOVERY SEMINAR

(For those experiencing any type of loss)

This seminar will help the participants:

- Prepare in advance for hurt, loss, and crisis

- Identify ungrieved losses

- Discover and implement the process of grief

- Understand the causes and recovery steps in trauma

- Understand what depression and anger are telling you

- Eliminate worry and anxiety from your life

- Learn a biblical perspective on loss and discover the comfort of God

- Learn how to say goodbye to what you have lost and move ahead in life

**For more information on scheduling
a seminar, call 1-800-875-7560.**

Helping Others at a Time of Loss, Crisis, and Trauma

(For ministers, therapists, lay counselors, graduate students, nurses)

Everyone in our country will experience their own personal Ground Zero at one time or another. Most people in our communities have never been given guidance on how to confront their everyday losses and grieve over them…so they carry burdens of pain and turmoil. This seminar will help people on the path to recovery. Ministers and counselors can become the hands of Christ in ministering to those within the church and outside the church. But *we* need to be equipped. That's the reason for this training experience.

In this seminar you will:

- Learn the various types of losses in life and the steps needed to recover

- Be given a step-by-step procedure to follow with actual statements to use in helping others at a time of loss

- Be given a very specific structure model of helping in both loss and crisis situations. (This will cover the stages of crisis and *What to Do* and *Say* at each stage)

- Observe how to help others in a time of loss, crisis, or trauma. Guidance will be given on what to do and say to assist others with their anger, depression, and anxiety

- Learn how to determine the strength of each person in crisis, what spiritual resources to use and apply, and when to apply them

- Learn how to identify unresolved issues from the past and the steps involved in recovery

- Be given suggestions on equipping every person in your church to handle loss and care for others

For more information on scheduling a seminar, call 1-800-875-7560.